Creative Crafts
for Children

Creative Crafts

for Children

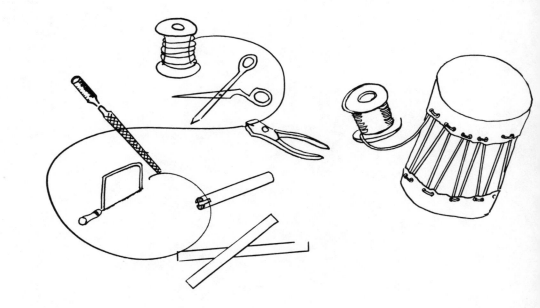

KENNETH R. BENSON
New York University

Illustrated by
EVELYN H. BENSON, designer

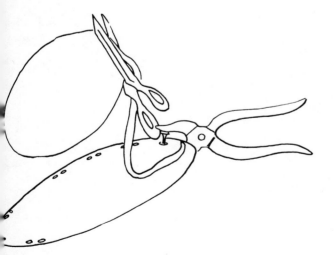

PRENTICE-HALL, INC.
Englewood Cliffs, N.J.

To
CRAIG AND DOREEN
AND COUNTLESS MILLIONS OF YOUNGSTERS

Foreword

Research indicates a need for a practical manual of crafts projects. This study, relating the leadership responsibilities of teachers, playground leaders and camp counselors to the craft activity needs of children, will be constructively helpful in craft activity situations.

Forty illustrated craft projects, complete with the step-by-step procedures necessary for the completion of each project, are included. Projects are arranged from the simple to the complex, thereby providing opportunity for leaders to select those projects which meet the specific needs of their programs.

Table of Contents

Projects

Projects

Projects

Projects

Creative Crafts
for Children

1 The place of crafts in school, camping, and playground programs

It is estimated that over 15,000,000 children take part in programs conducted on summer playgrounds and that almost 4,000,000 children have an organized camping experience every year in the United States. These large numbers of participants, to say nothing of the over 30,000,000 children in our schools, place a great responsibility not only on the individual leaders, but even to a greater degree on the principals, supervisors, and program planners. Within the grasp of these executives lie the potentialities for the further development of programs that will meet the needs of children in these situations. Comprehensive programs employing various media of expression with opportunity for choice of activity will provide the greatest contribution towards the growth and development of participating youngsters. These broad programs should not only have great breadth and depth within the framework of the total program but each individual activity should also possess these qualities to help maintain interest and provide a continuous challenge to the imagination and interest of the children.

During the past years crafts have become prominent in home activities, leisure time pursuits, and in school, camp, and playground programs. During the decade beginning in 1920, the number of playgrounds and camps increased by leaps and bounds. Programs that previously were heavily weighted with sports were expanded to include more creative activities. On playgrounds music, drama, arts and crafts, and nature activities received increasing emphasis.*

In recent years playgrounds and camps have become more than specialized areas of play. Educators and leaders in these fields have recognized the unique potentials of the environment and have further recognized the importance of programs that occur best in the natural setting and surroundings provided by well-planned camps and playgrounds. In these natural settings the normal development of youngsters is further implemented by providing activities that are both interesting and educationally sound.

Playgrounds and camp administrators have recognized the important position their respec-

---

* National Recreation Association, *Recreation and Park Yearbook*, 1950, p. 12.

1

tive programs are playing in the development of the youth of America. It is recognized that youngsters during this developmental period should be exposed to and encouraged to participate in many activities. The impact of this developmental stage of growth is of vital importance if we are to expect children to emerge from adolescence and enter adulthood with a solid background of exploratory experiences. These exploratory experiences are the framework upon which the structure of their future life is based.

Crafts now form an integral part of programs in schools, camps, and on playgrounds. In their various forms crafts are a method of communication between the brain cortex of an individual and his hand-eye coordination. The completed project represents the degree of coordination that existed while the thought and manipulative processes were combining. The scope of crafts is as broad as the range of materials, as deep and varied as the thought process, and as personal as are individual differences among people.

> From foil pictures to hollow ware
> From lanyards to leather saddles
> From Jersey loops to woven tapestries
> From scale models to furniture

This is the story of crafts.

On playgrounds and in camps where youngsters gather at their own volition through interest and desire to participate, crafts can well provide balance to programs that are generally heavily weighted with physical activities; sports, games, swimming, and other strenuous physical activities need to be counterbalanced with more creative, less physically exhausting activity. This interlacing of other media of expression with crafts provides an outlet for pent emotions, and for the release of tensions so often the result of highly competitive sport programs.

All youngsters have a creative spark that can, and should, be fanned into a flame. Young-

sters have ideas. It is the teacher's responsibility to help crystalize these ideas in the thinking and action of youngsters, and to open up new learning experiences. This capitalization on the creative spark of children through craft activities will aid in the unfolding of the personality of the participants and help develop latent talents and abilities. Quite frequently pre-vocational exploratory craft experiences provide leaders and teachers with a greater knowledge of a youngster's abilities, likes and dislikes, habits and attitudes. In light of this additional information, teachers and leaders obtain a clearer total picture of children and, therefore, can more ably provide guidance and help with these youngsters in their selection and pursuit of a vocation.

Children, too, get to know their abilities, talents, likes and dislikes. They begin to make decisions about materials, projects, choice and use of tools, selection of color combinations, and have the immediate chance to "try out" their ideas, thoughts, and choices of many kinds. They recognize their skills and can compare ideas, projects, and techniques using the crafts as the common denominator of thought, action, and conversation. Leadership, as well as the development of "followship" attributes, will develop and emerge in the youngsters as a result of the interaction of these children and craft activities.

Youngsters can develop a feeling of accomplishment and receive recognition as a result of craft activities. Craft projects completed on playgrounds and in camps and schools are one of the few items that remain as everlasting reminders of the joy of accomplishment. Craft items can be displayed in any appropriate location, while the home run or stolen base is remembered only until the next game. Youngsters will remember an outstanding athletic feat they have performed, but in crafts they have the three-dimensional item they have constructed to prove and show their skill.

2

Crafts can provide interesting activities for cabin, playground, or class groups during leisure time and during inclement weather when outdoor or excessively vigorous activities are impossible. The hot and humid days which are so prevalent during the summer months in many sections of the United States make it mandatory to include more passive, less taxing activities; crafts can admirably fill this gap in programming. In large cities children have little or no opportunity in their apartment dwellings to pursue craft activities or just "make things." Space in apartment living is at such a premium that the setting aside of a room or even a small closet for craft work and storage is almost an impossibility. The "dirt" resulting from these activities discourages parental permission, to say nothing of the noise and possible damage to furniture and other household equipment.

These restrictions placed on our youngsters, coupled with the absence of craft leadership, make it virtually impossible for children to pursue many of these craft activities in their dwellings. Rural living has fewer restrictions in the pursuit of crafts than urban living; however, the problem of the acquisition of needed supplies, tools, and equipment is frequently more difficult to solve. As in urban situations, the absence of trained craft leadership in the rural home is a deterrent to the pursuit of craft activities. Children need to be taught to achieve their maximum potential development. Crafts combine manual manipulations with mental challenge, thereby meeting the needs of youngsters for both manual dexterity and mental growth. Leaders are constantly on the alert for programs that educate and train the whole child. Craft experiences are an admirable way to achieve this end.

2 Organization of program

The planning of a crafts program for schools, playgrounds, and camps is based principally on the fundamental needs of children and their expressed desires and interests that can be satisfied by craft participation. Many factors combine in these situations which through their very nature have great influence upon the scope and breadth of craft programs. Leadership, facilities, equipment, tools, supplies and materials all have their influence on the outcome of craft programs. Balance between these areas of consideration is important. An inadequate supply of materials cannot be balanced by an overabundance of tools; certainly in this illustration the reverse would be preferable. However, the ideal would be to retain balance between materials and tools, as well as between the factors that determine the effectiveness of craft programs.

The greatest service camp directors, playground administrators, and principals can perform is to put in action those thoughts and ideas concerning craft programs that seem appropriate for the situation. Craft programs' worth and value have to be "sold" and explained in terms of the total program. Administrators and leaders can, and should, encourage participation by giving verbal endorsement as well as financial support on a basis equal with other activities.

It is an administrative function to continually strive to eliminate those things which may hinder the effectiveness of craft programs. Facilities should be made available and maintained in good condition. Tools should be kept sharp and in good repair. Materials and supplies should be made available by anticipating demands and requisitioning in sufficient quantities these needed items well in advance to insure their availability when the demand arises. Few things can be more discouraging or have a greater undesirable impact on craft programs than "running out" of needed materials. As a result projects remain incomplete, materials already used are wasted, teachers and leaders lose interest, and children become discouraged. At these early ages children should achieve success, for failure is a deep rooted scar that frequently through life is a detriment to participation.

Crafts can well serve as a trap to catch the fleeting interests of youngsters who, in the fashion of a honeybee, travel from opportunity to opportunity, taking and giving, but always remaining only so long as there is interest, opportunity, and challenge. Craft programs should be organized to trap these interests. In order to effectively accomplish this objective, programs should be made sufficiently flexible to permit youngsters to enter the craft group at any time and to immediately have the opportunity to take part. Long waiting periods required in some situations accomplish little more than loss of interest by the children in the activity, and the possible turning of their interest to some other less desirable activity.

Compact craft kits containing the necessary tools, supplies, and materials should be on hand in the camp and on the playground as well as the school. These kits can be checked out by teachers or leaders when the need arises. More than one kit of this type would most likely be needed in schools and a majority of camps and playground situations. It would be unreasonable to expect the average teacher to effectively handle more than fifteen to twenty youngsters at one time. However, some craft activities lend themselves more effectively to larger group participation than others. Variations in the effectiveness and previous craft experiences of the leaders will also modify the number of youngsters that can effectively be handled. Craft kits, therefore, should contain tools, materials, and supplies adequate to serve a maximum of twenty youngsters.

At the end of each day's use, craft kits should be checked closely at the point of distribution, be it the craft shop in camps and schools, or the administration building on playgrounds, to make certain that all tools are in good condition and all used materials and supplies are replaced. In all situations where more than one craft kit is used a color-marking code can be employed to prevent the mixing of tools between kits. Tools within a kit can be marked with the same color paint that is used to paint the inside and outside of the kit. This marking makes it possible to immediately distinguish one set of tools from another.

In situations where craft kits are ineffective due to their inability to carry a sufficient quantity of tools, materials, and supplies, craft wagons can be employed. These wagons can be designed to open and expose simple tool boards (*see* drawing on page 6), and to contain additional tools, materials, and supplies. Three-wheel wagons used frequently in cities to deliver groceries, laundry, etc., can well be used as the basic framework for these wagons. Additional construction will be required to make provisions for separate compartments containing the needed tools, materials, and supplies. As in the case of craft kits, craft wagons should be attractively painted with designs and motifs that will appeal to children, and be representative of the activity. One suggested possibility for decoration would be to paint the body of the wagon all white with red wheels, and tool silhouettes painted in black over the white background. An inventory of all tools should be posted on the inside to facilitate checking and closing out at the end of the activity. It is of utmost importance while employing either the craft kits or craft wagons to have a clearly identified and defined place for each tool, supply, and materials.

Storage of craft kits and craft wagons will not raise a great problem in schools. Any suitable room that is dry and under the control of a responsible person should suffice. These units should be accessible on immediate notice, making it mandatory that the person in charge of these kits be available at all times. If this central storage in schools makes for administrative problems due to unique situations, each craft class could be charged with a kit, keeping it in their room. On playgrounds and camps, kits could be stored either in the administrative building or in any building where sufficient space is available. On playgrounds where neither space nor buildings are available, craft kits either have to be delivered each day by car or truck to the playground leader and returned to a central location by the same method; or the various playground leaders may be held responsible for picking up and returning to a central location craft kits desired for that day's activity.

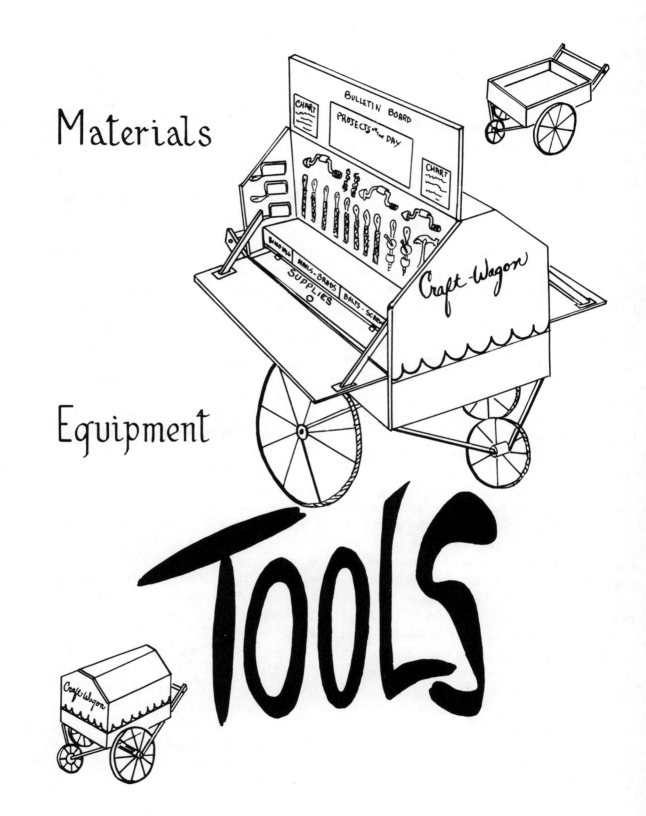

Materials

Equipment

TOOLS

Craft programs should be so organized as to make it possible for the teacher to give a clear, short, general demonstration at the start of each craft session. After the demonstration the leader or teacher should provide individual help and instruction. Projects should be so selected as to insure completion by the youngsters in one session. In view of the short interest span of younger children every effort should be made in organizing the craft program to make it possible, especially in the first few craft sessions, for children to complete one project during each session. Immediate success will encourage further interest and activity.

Provisions should be made for children having a greater sustained interest to become more involved in projects that require not only greater skill but longer time to complete. A project that might require three or four sessions for completion should not be discouraged by the leader. However, there should be real assurance on the part of the child as well as leader that the youngster will complete his undertaking. When a project is attempted every effort should be made on the part of the leader or teacher to insure its completion. It is, therefore, very important for leaders at the beginning to guide children into those projects that are simple and fairly easy to complete. While the child is so engaged judgments can be made regarding children in reference to their abilities, interest span, and how much help they require. These judgments can help the leader or teacher to guide children into those project areas that best serve the needs of the individual child.

Many craft leaders and teachers are not highly trained craft specialists. It is, therefore, even more important that they "feel" their way into the leading of craft programs. While it is generally desirable for youngsters to have a wide choice of projects, leaders with little training and experience in these programs should not attempt to provide unlimited project selection.

Children's interests and needs vary greatly. Therefore, it would be likely in a group of fifteen youngsters, with complete freedom of choice, that fifteen different project interests would be expressed. These projects could well encompass many material media. The problem of starting these youngsters in fifteen different projects simultaneously is an impossible task even for the most skillful leader. Two or three project possibilities within the material medium should be the maximum presented to the group. Although this method of presentation limits choice at the beginning, the leader has ample time and opportunity when the children are working to speak individually to each youngster. While so doing the children who finish their projects first can be individually helped in other project areas.

Leaders should be constantly aware of the pitfalls of having too many material media used simultaneously. This type of craft programming frequently requires special tools that are often unattainable and raises the problem of prolonged individual attention and instruction. The distribution of many more tools, supplies, and equipment imposes an extremely heavy burden on the leader with the loss of efficiency and continuity reducing the effectiveness of the program.

The following table indicates the cost of tools necessary to complete the projects illustrated in the Manual. Page 8 contains a photograph of these tools.

Tool requirements and costs for recommended craft projects.*

TOOL	COST	TOOL	COST
Brush, Artist #1	$ .10	Knife, X-acto #1	.55
Brush, ½″	.25	Linoleum Cutting Tools	1.50
Brush, 1″	.35	Needle, sewing	.05
Brush, Stencil	.10		
Brayer, 1″ dia. roller x 4″ wide	.75	Pencil	.05
		Pliers, Cutting, 6″	1.50
Can Opener	.25	Pliers, Slip Joint	.55
C-Clamp, 4″	.45	Rotary Punch	1.75
Compass, pencil	.15	Saw, Coping	.75
File, 6″ flat smooth	.50		
File, 6″ half-round smooth	.50	Saw, Coping	.75
		Saw, Hand, 20″, 10 points cross cut	2.50
Glass Cutter	.25	Saw, Keyhole	1.25
Hammer, Ball Peen (light)	.75	Scissors	1.00
Hammer, Claw (light)	1.60	Scratch Awl	.25
Hand Drill (¼″ capacity)	1.80	Screw Driver, 6″	.35
⅛″ Twist Drill	.15		
		Straight Pin	.00
¼″ Twist Drill	.35	Tin Snip, 10″	1.75
Knife, Sloyd	.60		
		TOTAL	**$23.70**

* Cost listed is that of medium-priced tools.

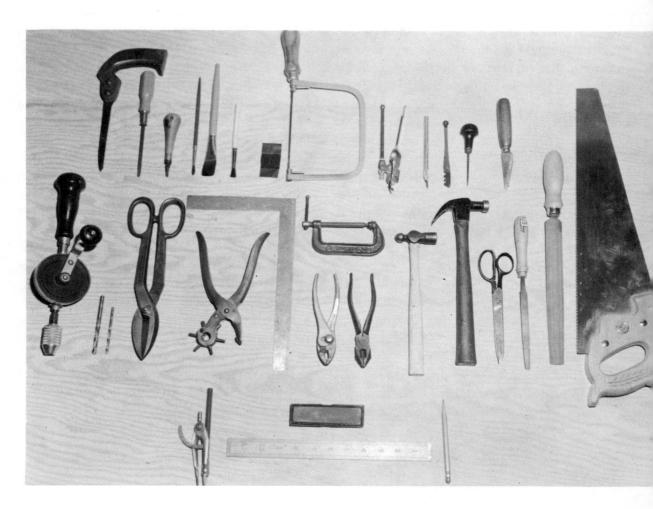

3 The basis for motivation

Children desire to create, build, and construct. Observation of a group of youngsters at the beach will indicate that although the refreshing coolness of the water brings joy and fun, seemingly greater pleasure is derived by the children using their hands to model and build in the moist sand. This creative release is more than just the fulfillment of a physical need to feel, grasp, and experiment. It involves the whole of the child. This combination of the physical and mental abilities of youngsters is naturally expressed in the crafts.

Motivation for the activity should include those things that are helpful to the youngsters in the realization of their objectives. The very nature of the activity is conducive to participation. Children should be helped to derive pleasure and fun as a result of this participation. Although perfection in the finished article should be encouraged at all times, it should not be the ultimate goal of the craft program.

Emphasis should be placed on personal satisfactions and creativity plus the joy of doing, rather than the attainment of perfection in the finished article. Craftsmanship should always be encouraged but not at the expense of participation. Youngsters quickly realize that the artificial goals created by misguided adult teachers and leaders are often beyond the grasp of the majority of the children. This realization of fact by the youngsters is one of the greatest deterrents to participation. To motivate youngsters, goals and objectives should be within the grasp of the children. These goals and objectives should be within the range of the skills and abilities the children possess, and should at all times be flexible enough to permit variations for individual differences. Standardized goals for all youngsters are both impractical and impossible if participation and satisfaction by all youngsters is desired. Minimum or maximum standards of project performance should be set for individuals and not for groups.

It is highly desirable for teachers and leaders to motivate children by encouraging and expressing personal interest in the child, as well as in the project the youngster is constructing. One of the most rewarding human experiences that a youngster can participate in—crafts in all its ramifications—has the possibility of motivating children in other broad program areas of exploration.

Children and adults are constantly striving to gain recognition and status within their social groups. Children are constantly desiring and trying to gain status in a society, based on adult concepts and regulations. Crafts can provide children with the opportunity to successfully compete with adults, and as a result of this competition gain recognition in this society.

Crafts projects completed on playgrounds and in camps and schools provide children with the opportunity to "carry home" the result of their participation. The results of participation in other program areas are far more difficult to display or show. The home run, or a perfect drive are but a few examples of the many things that may happen to a child while participating in a total program; however, craft projects are one of the few items that can be carried home as a reminder for reliving an eventful day. Parents, teachers, and the community can better evaluate the participation of children in crafts as a result of seeing the various projects that have been constructed. This evaluation of the craft program by the community through the finished article is quite normal for the lay person. However, teachers and leaders should be more concerned with what the material has done for the child, and not what the child has done with the material.

Craft fairs, displays, and shows all have a definite place in the motivation of craft programs. These exhibits of craft projects provide the children with the recognition that comes from pointing with pride to their own creation. The joy of realization that their project is on exhibit, and is making a contribution to the total display, helps to motivate children into doing bigger and greater things. The exchange of ideas that results from projects attractively displayed in a single setting still further motivates them by stressing in the finished article the value of careful planning, need for further skill, and the importance of craftsmanship.

Individual children's projects should be brought to the attention of the whole craft group. This can be accomplished by holding up the project high enough so that all can see. At the same time some desirable feature should be found in each project. Choice of color or color combinations, design, or skill of execution should also be brought to the attention of the whole group. All projects completed that day should receive this recognition. While the teacher is commenting on the various aspects of the completed projects a golden opportunity for further suggestions presents itself in guiding children to those crafts areas in which their demonstrated skills and abilities would most likely provide the greatest opportunity for success.

If a child finds it very difficult to capture detail he should be guided at this stage of his development into a craft or project in which fine detail is not a prerequisite to success. At the same time this craft or project should be a challenge to his imagination and should not merely be a repetition of what he has already done. A small display or exhibit of completed projects should be set up either by cabin groups or craft groups at the end of each week, or when an ample supply of projects are available to make an attractive and adequate display.

This exhibit should be for the participants of other activity areas or cabin groups to promote wider interest in the crafts. The exhibit could be set up on work benches, picnic tables, or folding tables with provision made for some protective guard rails constructed with a rope railing to prevent loss and spectator handling. To further insure the safety of the items a youngster, or several youngsters, from the craft group should stand by to see that the spectators observe the exhibit regulations. These youngsters can also serve as guides and information centers for questions that always arise as the result of displays of this type.

Teachers and leaders should take the time to photograph craft exhibits and to distribute copies of these photographs to local newspapers. Articles accompanying these photographs should briefly explain the background of the photographs and give credit to the participating youngsters.

4 The need for creativity

Children naturally express themselves, using symbolic representations of things they are interested in and are familiar with. A line constructed with a blue crayon on a drawing forms in the imagination of the child the blue horizon, while trees may be represented by a series of green lines. Provided that the opportunity arises, there is little doubt that these symbols could well become a design for a specific craft project. This practical application of the creative potential of youngsters engages the whole of their intellectual and physical powers, and provides an outlet for their imagination.

Creativity is inherent to a greater or less degree in all people. It is expressed to a greater extent by those individuals who are first familiar with the medium, its characteristics, modes of design, and potentialities. The great artists, craftsmen, engineers, and inventors of our civilization are outstanding examples of individuals who have developed creativity within themselves to a high perfection. Creativity, in its simple form, may be an idea, thought, movement, or a rearrangement of existing combinations of ideas, thoughts, or movements. In its more complicated form creativity may be considered the application of abstract thinking to ideas, thoughts, or movements.

Creativity is not to be confused with accidental discovery, but certainly creativity is present in one of its highest forms when the scientific processes are used to aid in the culmination of an invention. To be creative an individual need not be an inventor, nor discover or contribute any new concepts to society. He needs only to participate in a new way in an activity he has not previously experienced.

Frequently creativity is not in evidence in a completed project, even to a trained observer. However, great creativity might have taken place *within the individual* during the planning and execution of the project. So long as the individual has expressed his thoughts, ideas, and concepts in a physical way, be it vocal, by facial expression, or by the use of the hands and if these combinations are the individual's "own," he is experiencing creativity. One result of participation in crafts will be the production of a project; however, to society this project may contain little or no creative value, but to the individual constructing this project great creativity might well be expressed. If the individual has not previously constructed the project using the same techniques and procedures, high creative growth within the individual is possible.

The construction by children of very simple craft projects could well form the foundation

11

for the development of the creative experience. Any repetition of a single project using identical operations and processes is less likely to provide the possibility for creative experiences. To duplicate the prototype constructed by the same individual is little more than duplication of previous action, and is not very creative.

While the construction of a lanyard by a person might be a desirable project, the continued mass production of identical units by the same individual contributes little more than development of higher skill during the making of the first few. After the skill is so developed, little or nothing is gained by additional construction. It is not twenty projects experienced but rather one project experienced twenty times over. While the making of these lanyards may provide recreation in its broad form it is a limited experience.

Frequently teachers and leaders prefer having youngsters participate in those activities which they have already mastered. Little help is therefore needed by the children and the leader or teacher is less likely to be *bothered* by questions. Teachers and leaders could, and should, provide additional learning experiences.

As in the case of lanyard-making, color, different weaves, endings, and other variations could be introduced leading to other uses of "lanyard material." Earrings, ornamental pins, and bracelets are but a few of the many project possibilities within this material medium. Knowledge of the many variations and usages of the material opens the way for the informed to create still newer combinations, and to apply his newly-found knowledge and skill to further increase his creative ability.

5 Group projects

Single projects that involve one or more persons may serve many desirable ends, especially when these projects are planned by the action of the group and when they serve the particular needs of the group. Frequently interest in crafts may be stimulated through the other program areas. The dramatic group might require simple costumes that could be constructed with the help of the craft group. The exchange of ideas and the rendering of mutual help by both groups contributes to the total program.

Crafts classes should not be expected as a result of the nature of the activity to provide building or maintenance service for the other activities. However, if the craft group desires to help design and build flats for a play, this cooperative action should be encouraged and implemented by the leadership of both the craft and dramatic groups. This coordination between program areas helps integrate the total program at the same time it helps youngsters correlate in their minds the place and importance of crafts in life situations. As a result of group craft projects, children see and feel the impact of group actions—and the necessity for group cooperation in order to achieve worthwhile results. These experiences in group craft projects have carry-over value for everyday living and life adjustment in a democracy.

Caution should always be exercised in the planning and execution of these cooperative ventures. All children involved should have clearly defined responsibilities based on their interests and level of skill. Teachers and leaders responsible for the conduct of group projects in crafts should be ever mindful that children to a large degree are interested in crafts because they can make something that is their own.

Ownership to children is important; and leaders can, through explanation and example, demonstrate that no single individual could have had the time or possess the ability to create the group project, but by each giving a little of his talents the group created something bigger and better than could have been accomplished by any individual working alone.

Group craft projects frequently are engaged in by children as a result of interest in other program areas. A kite-flying contest with the kites being constructed by groups, each kite representing a special interest group within the total program, is but one example of a group project.

6 Making the activity safe

No program, however excellent otherwise, can be considered a real success if an accident resulting in serious injury or death occurs to any of the participants, or to a teacher or leader. It therefore behooves the leaders of these activities to take early notice of conditions favoring accidents, and to do all possible to promote safe conduct of activities. It is the purpose of this section of the manual to call attention to the need for safety, the benefits derived from its practice, and to enumerate certain hazards that must be taken into consideration.

It is assumed that the teacher or leader will, by description, explanation, example, and understanding, make a real attempt to instill safety consciousness into his charges. This instruction is just as important as the teaching of specific skills, ideas, or concepts related to the area of learning. Safety should be taught in conjunction with the content of the specific area of learning.

BENEFITS OF A SAFETY CAMPAIGN

The long-term benefits of a safety campaign, carried on with such vigor as to get the idea or the outlook implanted into the children, may be very great. Aside from the satisfaction derived from the knowledge that safety is being taught, children who learn to apply the principles to their everyday tasks and to their unsupervised time will have acquired an aid in their protection throughout their lives. Further, safety requires observation and often study. Sometimes, it only calls for one to think for a moment. But these habits of observation and of stopping to think may well be applied to any normal problem, not only to avoid danger, but also to promote success. The point is that a real desire to operate in a safe manner may simply bring a pause for thought which in turn insures the operational success of the task. Safety is a habit and attitude the development of which should be encouraged.

HAZARDS

A hazard is defined as a condition that has the potential of being dangerous and which may cause injury to the unwary. Hazards can be broadly separated into three classes—natural, mechanical, and personal. For example, a steep cliff is a natural hazard; a dull or broken

14

tool is a mechanical hazard. Frequently little can be done to eliminate the natural hazards. Small natural hazards can easily be overcome; by preparation and understanding nearly all natural hazards can be prevented from causing injury. Mechanical hazards can practically, by definition, be eliminated. These will be treated in more detail later.

The third class of danger potential or personal hazard is man himself. Teachers and leaders will from time to time encounter individuals who seem to generate accidents without any help from physical objects. Such persons are sometimes called accident prone, and are referred to herein as personal hazards.

To assist teachers and leaders in making quick appraisals of the safety conditions in a camp, playground, or school area, a discussion of typical hazards is given below. Where it is within the teacher's and leader's province to take action offsetting the danger, such action is outlined.

Natural Hazards

Weather conditions such as wind, excessive rain, lightning, sunburn, frostbite, etc. are always with us. These cannot be dangerous except by their effects. Yet, how would a leader know that the area selected for a summer activity could be flooded and washed away by excessive rain? How would he know that high trees could be sent crashing onto the group by hurricane or tornado winds? Would he realize that lightning danger is unusually great in a given area? These are the kinds of hazards about which inquiry should be made. The local authorities will usually have as good information as can be found. While little can be done about the danger, an instructor facing an activity area where such conditions prevail should have a sound plan of protection or evacuation for his charges in case of difficulties.

Again, in rural camp areas, the general na-

ture of the terrain should be noted. Existence of steep cliffs, deep or fast-moving water, high-speed highways should be known to the leaders, and proper precautions taken. Existence of poisonous weeds or plants, poisonous snakes, wild animals, insects, and the like that can result in injury cannot be ignored.

In urban areas, the natural hazards described above are not so likely to be found, but whether urban or rural, the instructor or leader should take note of conditions and act to forestall any accidents resulting therefrom.

Wooded areas are sometimes subject to serious grass or brush fires. Leaders should recognize the consequences of such a disaster in a summer camp area.

At the risk of seeming repetitious, it must be stated again that natural hazards, as outlined above, can hardly be eliminated. Therefore, about the only course of action available to the instructor is to see that his charges appreciate the dangers that may lurk unseen. It is recommended that an early explanation be given to the youngsters on this subject. A field trip, under close supervision, to areas where hazards exist, may serve to fix safety ideas in the young minds. A contest, wherein a small prize is given to the student or students who describe some of the dangerous situations most accurately, may instill an eagerness to avoid danger. In fact, throughout the school, camp, and playground session, if it can be made a matter of public notice or even praise whenever a student exercises good judgment in avoiding danger or operating in a safe manner, great help may be given the whole safety program. Needless to say, the teacher and leader must go out of his way to emphasize his own attitude toward safety. *Much progress is made by example.*

Mechanical Hazards

Mechanical hazards, for the purpose of this discussion, are all those dangers associated

15

with the tools, equipment, materials, playground devices, and the like, which the students normally use in the course of working, learning, or playing.

Here, the instructor must outline the orderly steps that promote safe sessions, and this outline must be integrated into the subject matter without undue stress. In other words, safety and accident prevention should be made a natural part of any camp or playground activity, and it is the leader or instructor who can work in this idea in an unobtrusive fashion. Detailed considerations are discussed below.

A primary consideration is the working area. It must be clean, level, well lighted, sheltered from the weather, and so on. In this category cleanliness and good housekeeping are of paramount importance, since the mere act of establishing order in these respects will automatically bring about other corrective measures that improve safety conditions. Next in order are the tools that are used. These should be in good condition, sharp, and essentially able to perform as well as new. They should be adequate in number. Students should not try to carry on operations with tools not designed for such operations. The instructor should carefully organize his session to accommodate his tool and material supply.

Tools should be checked daily. To carry out this task, the program organization should provide for a routine system of distributing tools as well as work material. In the reverse procedure, that is, where tools are returned to tool box or craft wagon, a good opportunity for inspection exists. Depending on the age and responsible attitude of the students, they may be employed to assist in all safety inspection procedures. However, this will not normally relieve the instructor of the duties of over-all inspections.

Mechanical power tools, such as drills, saws, grinders, and the like, should be operated by the instructor if the students are quite young.

Older students, or those showing unusual mechanical aptitude or safety consciousness, may be allowed to operate such devices under close supervision. Here is an area in which the instructor should meticulously observe all safety practices, such as face shield, goggles, rolled up sleeves, tucked in neckties, good lights, tool guards, ventilating systems, belt guards, dry floors, good electrical cords, grounded equipment, and so forth. It is well to have a standing arrangement with the students for safety checking, with a word of praise or honorable mention for any youngster who calls attention to the omission of any safety act.

Despite all efforts to avoid accidents, it must be recognized that one may occur; therefore, the work area should have a properly stocked first aid kit.

Do not overlook the danger of fire, or of students being overcome by paint or lacquer fumes or smoke. The work area, particularly where lacquers or solvents are employed, in addition to being well ventilated, should contain fire extinguishers and fire blankets, and the instructor should know how to practice one of the methods of artificial respiration. Such knowledge will also apply in case a student should be on the verge of drowning.

Hazards arising from the use of materials are probably most difficult to point out. The most usual accidents are cuts or abrasions from sharp edges left on metal, glass, ceramics, etc., by other tool operations. Usually it is not the cut itself that is so important as the possible danger of later infection. Youngsters must be encouraged to seek first aid for even minor injuries, and here again the leader must be the first to display his safety attitude by bandaging minor injuries.

Injuries to the eye should be regarded as major, and should receive immediate professional medical attention.

In respect to general medical attention, the instructor or leader should at the earliest possible moment in setting up a camp or playground find out the names and locations of at least three general practitioners so that medical attention can be secured with minimum delay when needed. In schools this information is available in the office.

Personal Hazard

For want of a better term, personal hazard is applied to those individuals who seem to be prone to accidents. These hazards are by far the hardest to overcome. The outward manifestation of accident proneness is usually great clumsiness and an inability to hold tools properly or handle them effectively. There is often a complete *mental void* about danger, dangerous situations, or accidents. There is another type of personal hazard individual who deliberately flouts safety rules, showing how he can get by without observing them.

Of the various types of individuals listed above, the latter can be subject to disciplinary action and dismissal from the session. In fact, the instructor should adopt this stern course at once, because such individuals may draw around them a set of disciples and wreak havoc with the safety program for the entire session.

The other personal hazards, those who are clumsy, nonmechanical, nonsafety minded, deserve patient treatment by the instructor. A first step is a check on their general health, including eyesight, hearing, muscular coordination, etc. Next, a few checks on their mental levels, to see whether they really do understand instructions.

If health and educational levels are satisfactory, about the only courses open to the instructor are private sessions to attempt to improve their safety abilities, together with *judicious placing of these individuals in the session to avoid undue hazards.* If there is no improvement, it may simply have to be recognized that these individuals are poorly placed in a school,

camp, or playground activity, and would be subject to less danger in other environments. Usually, however, a health check up will show the reason for the trouble and point the way to some corrective measures.

Be sure school, camp, or playground area has a telephone, or know where to find one quickly. Always keep a car or truck with a tank full of gasoline to permit emergency trips at night when gasoline stations may be closed. Keep a supply of flashlights, batteries, and bulbs. Do not use candles for emergency lighting. Washing facilities should be available; cleanliness is a desirable habit to develop.

The very nature of some craft activities is such as to require protection of clothing. If cloth aprons are not available, several sheets of newspaper held in place with a piece of string and tied tightly about the waist will serve as a suitable substitute. The protection of clothing not only reduces the possibility of soiling but also aids in the realization on the part of the children that cleanliness is of prime importance in the development of safe working habits.

Orderly and systematic procedures should be followed in the distribution of tools. These procedures should be routine and carefully executed to avoid the milling around of youngsters while carrying sharp tools. Each youngster should have a "work station" with ample room for movement. Avoid overcrowding. Leaders should never tolerate "horseplay" while craft activities are being conducted. Discipline must be maintained and enforced at all times.

The following table indicates some shop accident facts that may provide greater insight into the problem of accident prevention. While this table is primarily concerned with accidents involving shop activities, leaders of craft programs may glean from this table information relative to their specific situations and become more conscious of the need for safety.

Shop accident facts.*

ACCIDENT FREQUENCY	CONDITIONS OF RELATIVE FREQUENCY
By the time of day	⅗ occur in morning, ⅖ in afternoon. Highest frequency during hour after 10 A.M.
By day of week	Highest frequency on Wednesday.
By month of year	Highest frequency during early and late months of year. Also high just prior to, and following, vacation period.
By age of student	Marked increase in frequency at age 14, reaching peak at age 15.
By area of activity	Hazardous work areas, as determined by frequency of accidents: woods, metals, transportation, communication, and graphic arts. (Most hazardous—woods.)
By hand tool	Higher frequency of accidents in use of wood chisel than all other tools combined. Other tools classified as especially dangerous: saw, knife, plane, hammer, file, and soldering iron.
By machine tool	Hazardous machines, as determined by frequency of accidents: jointer, circular saw, wood lathe, grinder, band saw, drill press, engine lathe.
Machine tool versus hand tool	Hand tool accidents twice as numerous as machine tool accidents. Machine tool accidents more serious.
By size of class	Accidents tend to increase with shop enrollments, up to 25, then the number of accidents decreases as size of class continues to increase.
By experience of student	First few weeks of experience most dangerous period.
By intelligence	Relationship between intelligence and accidents is in inverse ratio. Strong tendency of lower intelligence groups to be accident repeaters.

* Hughes, Wayne P., *Safety Procedures in the School Shop*, Doctor's Thesis. New York, N. Y.: New York University, p. 396.

7 Awards and evaluation

While in some program areas the presentation of awards for outstanding achievement may possibly serve some objective, the crafts program has in the carefully completed project and within the individual its own compensations and rewards. The youngster who wins the hundred yard dash needs a ribbon or award to relive his achievement. In crafts his completed project is a testimonial to his skill and accomplishment.

Craft contests, where individuals are judged on the basis of their completed projects, have no common denominator for comparison. No fair criteria for evaluation have yet been devised which would make it possible to compare one project against another. This is especially true if projects are compared that involve different materials, designs, and where functions are varied. If the creativeness of the project is the criterion, how does a judge determine which project is more creative, when the judge's background and experience are apt to be quite dissimilar from the maker's? In situations where a youngster's project is evidently far superior in all respects, is anything gained by compounding recognition and presenting the youngster with an additional reward? This gifted child is probably the member of the group least needing encouragement, as his achievement quite evidently speaks for itself.

It might be well to ask ourselves this question. If the child were to make a choice between the award and the project, which one would he choose to keep? The conclusion imposed must be based on the assumption that the award's financial worth is within bounds of reason. Teachers and leaders should be concerned with the effect of the activity on the child, rather than devote undue emphasis to what effect the child has on the material.

8 Projects

The following forty craft projects range from the very simple to the more complex. Within this range of project ideas teachers and leaders can select those projects that best meet the specific requirements of their participants, as well as their requirements of their program. Generally, younger children can be expected to construct those projects that are listed first, while older children can build those projects that are presented later in this manual.

To facilitate instruction, leaders should construct all projects that are to be introduced into the program. This prior construction of projects by the leaders will help eliminate pitfalls that frequently arise when new projects are introduced.

Aluminum Foil Modeling

Tools

1. Scissors   2. Artist's brush   3. Pencil

Materials and Supplies

1. Aluminum foil
2. Pipe cleaners (if desired)
3. Oil paints (if desired)
4. Rubber cement
5. String or ribbon (if desired)

Procedure

The simplicity of working this material coupled with its wide adaptability provides youngsters with unlimited possibilities for extending their imagination in the building of their own three-dimensional figures. Simply take a sheet of foil and model it as one would model wet sand or clay.

The illustration shows a clown constructed by wadding and rolling aluminum foil. With scissors cut up the center to form legs. With colored ribbon or string tie at the ankles, waist, and neck. To form a large collar cut an extra sheet of aluminum foil and rubber-cement around neck. To form hands rubber-cement two thicknesses of foil together and cut out hands. With pencil make hole through figure at shoulder line; in hole place pipe cleaner, and on each end of pipe cleaner attach hands with rubber cement. Using small artist's brush and oil paint, paint features of clown.

A DELIGHT . . .
every way you use it!

Quick-Craft

Aluminum foil can easily be used for party decorations, any type of gift wrapping and even in time for the arrival of Santa Claus.

This cheerful circus clown with the oversized hands --- a place card favor or a decoration --- beckons you to the party table. Made from aluminum foil, the basic design can be easily adapted to fit any holiday celebration. Set off on your own and see what variations you can come up with.

Plaster of Paris Pins

Tools

1. Artist's brush
2. Knife

Materials and Supplies

1. Mixing container (paper cup or tin can)
2. Plaster of Paris
3. Water
4. Tempera paints
5. Shellac
6. Wax paper
7. Safety pin

Procedure

Pour one-half cup of water into mixing container, slowly add plaster of Paris until water no longer absorbs plaster. Stir with small stick. When consistency of mixture is that of whipped cream take a small amount of mixture on mixing stick and drop on a piece of wax paper. Continue making these forms until plaster is consumed. Each form will vary in size and design. Paint with tempera as the forms suggest: animals, birds, or faces.

When tempera paint is dry coat surface with thin coat of white shellac. When shellac is dry remove painted plaster form from wax paper and with a knife cut a groove in back of plaster form. Set the back of a safety pin in this groove and glue with Duco cement.

Play it Smart

. . . and make these custom-made pins to match any outfit, or bedeck any hat, purse, glove or shoe. After taking minutes to make, all you have to do is pin or sew them on permanently. Trim in seconds and wear all year.

Be a little more imaginative and even make a dainty necklace to match.

Have fun and try it now!

Plaster Paris

Red Tempra

Blue Tempra

Shellac

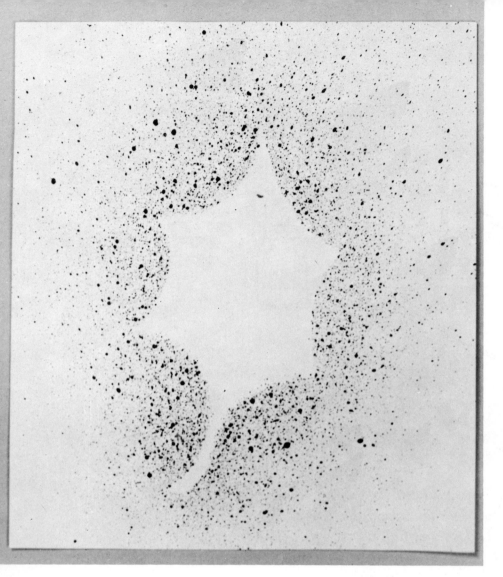

*Spatter
Prints*

Tools

1. Stencil brush or discarded tooth brush

Materials and Supplies

1. Construction paper
2. Tree or plant leaf

3. Tempera paints
4. Small piece of wire screening

Procedure

Place leaf or leaves (more than one can be used at the same time) flat on a piece of construction paper. Hold piece of wire screening about six inches above leaf and with a small amount of tempera paint on stencil brush paint over screen. As the bristles of the brush snap from wire to wire on screen, small specks of paint will be thrown on exposed portions of the construction paper, thereby forming a leaf design. Remove leaf or leaves and use designed paper as desired. Other designs can be *"created"* by cutting out forms from construction paper. These forms can be used in the place of leaves.

24

Springtime Magic

Pinwheels

Tools

1. Scissors
2. Ruler
3. Pencil
4. Punch

Materials and Supplies

1. One piece of construction paper
2. Straight pin
3. Small bead
4. ½" dowel

Procedure

Employing pencil and ruler construct a seven-inch square on construction paper. In this square draw two diagonals. Using scissors cut out square. Cut from each corner along the diagonal a distance of three inches. Punch a small hole one-half inch in from the edges of each of the right hand angles of the four triangles created by the diagonals.

Moving about the square in a clockwise direction, lift the corner of each triangle that has been punched toward the center of the square; insert a straight pin through the four holes. This pin is then forced through the center of the square and a small bead is threaded on the back of the pin. The pin is gently forced into a dowel or stick.

This is a Cinch

7.

6.

5.

1.

7"

7"

2.

3"

3.

1/2"

4.

Flashlight Faces

Tools

1. Scissors   2. Artist's brush (if desired)   3. Pencil

Materials and Supplies

1. Two-cell flashlight
2. Masking tape or string
3. Tempera paints and/or construction paper
4. Number four paper bag

Procedure

Obtain an unused #4 paper bag (a used paper bag is likely to be wrinkled and therefore difficult to use). Bulb end of flashlight is inserted two inches in open end of bag. Draw open end of bag together around flashlight and tape with masking tape or tie with string. Bag may be decorated by using tempera paints and/or construction paper. If tempera paints are used the design is drawn and painted directly on at least one of the faces of the bag (if desired, designs can be placed on all four sides of the paper bag).

If construction paper is used, the desired portions of the designs are cut out of this paper and rubber-cemented to one or more faces of the bag. While the picture on the paper bag is being designed the flashlight can be lighted in a darkened area to obtain the desired effect. Combinations of two or more faces can be used for dramatic skits.

For all the kids

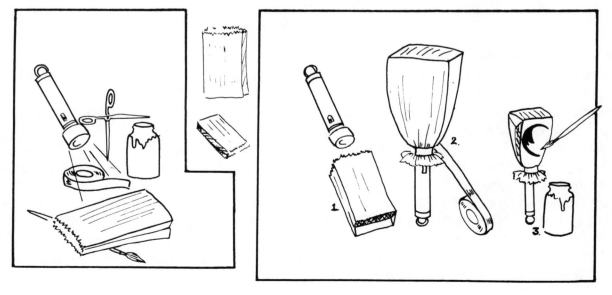

Plaster of Paris Picture Frames

Tools

1. Scissors
2. Pencil
3. Ruler
4. 1" brush

Materials and Supplies

1. Paper party plates
2. Discarded magazines
3. Plaster of Paris
4. Water
5. Mixing container
6. Hairpins
7. Fine sandpaper
8. Shellac

Procedure

Select an attractive, colored picture from a magazine or newspaper. Cut out picture so that it fits exactly in the flat inside bottom portion of a paper plate. If the bottom of the paper plate is a circle the picture should be cut out in the form of a circle, and if the bottom of the plate is square, the picture should be cut out to form a square of the same size. Place cut out picture *face down* inside and on bottom of paper plate. Mark location of top of picture on outside edge of paper plate.

Place a quantity of water approximately equal to the capacity of the paper plate in a mixing container. Slowly add plaster of Paris to the water until it no longer absorbs the plaster of Paris. With a stick stir the mixture. Carefully fill paper plate with mixture. Keep picture flat on bottom of plate. Insert hairpin in plaster so that bent end sticks out of plaster one-half inch (hairpin is used at top of picture to hang picture).

When plaster becomes warm, tear party plate from solid form. Picture will be framed in plaster of Paris. Smooth with sandpaper all rough edges and coat picture and frame with shellac.

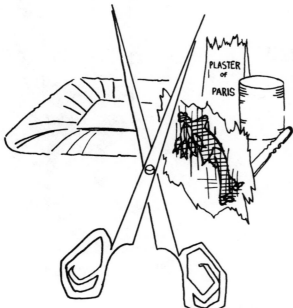

YOU'LL CHEER THIS . . .

simple and novel way of framing pictures of your own choice.

Decorate the walls of your home or club house in this inexpensive and effective manner. Pictures obtained from newspapers and magazines provide ample material for subjects.

Paper plates of assorted sizes and shapes make the basic forms while plaster of Paris carries out the theme.

Paper Bag Puppets

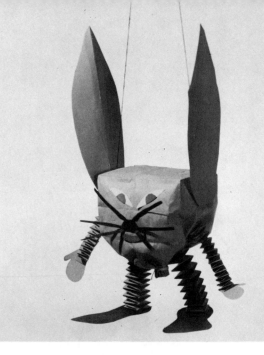

Tools

1. Scissors
2. Ruler
3. Pencil

Materials and Supplies

1. Construction paper 12″ x 18″
2. Number two paper bag
3. Several sheets of newspaper
4. String
5. Rubber cement

Procedure

Wad up several sheets of newspaper and stuff in paper bag until bag is three-quarters full. Draw open ends of bag together and tie with string.

To construct the arms cut four strips of construction paper five-eighths by 18 inches long. Overlap and cement at right angles to each other the ends of two of these strips. (For best results when cementing use rubber cement. Apply a thin coat of rubber cement to each surface to be joined. Permit both surfaces to dry, then bring these surfaces in contact with each other; lightly press the cemented joint.)

Place joined pieces flat on table. Using the strip that is on the bottom of the overlap, bend at edge of top strip back and over itself and press flat against overlap. Take second strip and bend at edge of first strip back and over itself, and press flat against overlap. Continue with alternate strips until entire length of construction paper is used. Cement last folds of paper together. Construct other arm in same manner.

For legs, cut four strips of construction paper one inch wide and 18 inches long. Using two strips of paper for each leg construct the legs in the same manner as the arms.

Using construction paper cut out ears, eyes, nose, and mouth, and cement in their proper place on the stuffed paper bag. On each side of the bag cement an arm. Spread out the surplus edges of the top of the bag to form a skirt, and under this skirt cement the two legs. Cut out construction paper hands and feet and cement in their proper positions.

Attach thin string to body of puppet behind each ear and/or attach strings to hands and feet.

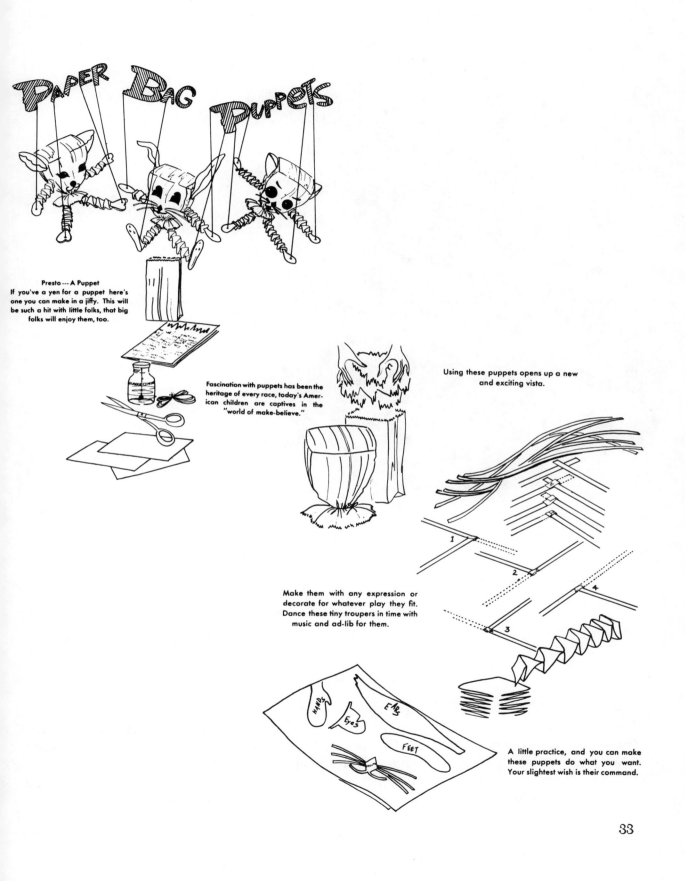

Paper Bag Puppets

Presto --- A Puppet
If you've a yen for a puppet here's one you can make in a jiffy. This will be such a hit with little folks, that big folks will enjoy them, too.

Fascination with puppets has been the heritage of every race, today's American children are captives in the "world of make-believe."

Using these puppets opens up a new and exciting vista.

Make them with any expression or decorate for whatever play they fit. Dance these tiny troupers in time with music and ad-lib for them.

HANDS
Eyes
EARS
FEET

A little practice, and you can make these puppets do what you want. Your slightest wish is their command.

Felt Hats

Tools

1. Scissors
2. Sewing needle
3. Pencil
4. Ruler

Materials and Supplies

1. Discarded fedora
2. Sewing thread
3. As desired: buttons, beads, sequins, etc.

Procedure

Obtain discarded fedora hat and remove lining, hat, and sweat bands. Using scissors cut completely around the hat at the point where brim joins the crown. This cutting will remove the crown from the brim. Completely around the edge of the crown construct with pencil and ruler a series of V's that are approximately three-quarters of an inch deep. Cut out V's with scissors. Turn up one and one-half inch of brim. Sew on colored buttons, pins, sequins, or beads as desired. Club insignia and emblems may also be used.

34

Just the thing
for **boys** (and girls, too)

1.

2.

3.

4.

5.

6. ←TURN UP

7.

Carnation Flowers

Tools

1. Pliers (if wire is used)

Materials and Supplies

1. Cleansing tissues (Kleenex)
2. 24-gauge wire (or bobbie pins)
3. Florist or ½" masking tape (if desired)
4. Pin-back or safety pin (if desired)
5. Powdered tempera

Procedure

Fold one cleansing tissue in half in the opposite direction to the regular fold lines. From one end of folded tissue to the other, make a series of accordion pleats about one-half inch wide. Press these pleats together. Over the center place a bobbie pin or a piece of 24-gauge wire that has been bent in the shape of a hairpin—if wire is used. Twist ends together. With fingers tear three-quarters of an inch from each end and spread the ends. Separate the top layer of the tissue and bring it up to the center. Separate the second layer and bring it up toward the center but not as far as the first layer. Separate third and fourth layers but do not bring up fourth layer. Spread out a thin layer of *dry* tempera powder on paper and gently rotate flower in powder in order to tint edges of tissue. Bobbie pin or wire stem can be taped with florist or masking tape. When taping, a pin-back or safety pin can be secured to stem in order to secure carnation flower to clothing.

The Crowning Touch

If you are in search of beauty try this delicate creation. Can be done in any color cleansing tissue, such as pastel blue, or pink, or even try a combination. Add fashions final touch through the magic of these colorful flowers.

A sonata in wire and tissue.

Utility Baskets

Tools

1. Knife   2. 1" paint brush   3. Artist's brush

Materials and Supplies

1. Oil paints
2. Fine sandpaper

3. Round or flat plastic lacing (if desired)

Procedure

Obtain from local grocery or vegetable store a basket of desired size and shape. Baskets range from the one-pint size (strawberries) up to bushel baskets (potatoes). With knife trim any loose or broken strips. Sandpaper any rough edges. Decide on color basket is to be painted and paint with oil paint.

Further decoration of basket may be accomplished by stenciling designs with oil paints on appropriate parts of basket (*see* section on stenciling). Decals may also be used for decorations. Handles may be wrapped with round or flat plastic lacing, which will add a decorative quality.

All

from DISCARDED BASKETS

IMAGINATION and PAINT

Plaster Sculpture

Tools

1. Knife 2. Artist's brush 3. 1″ paint brush

Materials and Supplies

1. Tempera paints
2. Plaster of Paris
3. Water

4. Shellac
5. Fine sandpaper
6. Paper cup

Procedure

Using a paper cup or half-pint milk container (larger milk containers could be used) fill milk container or paper cup with water. Pour water into mixing container (tin can will do) and slowly add plaster of Paris until water no longer absorbs the plaster; stir with stick. Fill paper cup or half-pint milk container with mixture. When outer surface of container becomes warm, carefully tear container from hardened plaster. Using knife carve desired form. Lightly sandpaper the surface and paint if desired with tempera paints; permit to dry, then shellac, using long brush strokes (do not brush too much as the colors will run). Exercise a high degree of control over group as the cuttings from the plaster of Paris are difficult to remove, even with a scraping-tool, from floors and tables.

Ever make plaster sculpture?

Now! Sculpture opportunities with inexpensive materials. Keep your program up to date, by incorporating this lively project idea. Just watch the eager way children take to this wonderful craft. They will love the effects. Take it from the interest of youngsters . . . it's sculpture time!

Driftwood

Tools

1. Knife
2. Fine sandpaper
3. 1" paint brush

Materials and Supplies

1. Flat oil paint
2. Tubes of powered metallic colors: copper, aluminum, green
3. White shellac

Procedure

Secure a piece of driftwood and place in sun to dry out. When dry, scrape all loose particles from surface (a wire brush is sometimes helpful). Lightly sandpaper and apply a very thin coat of white paint. In the recessed areas of the wood apply a thin coat of black paint. For applying both colors, use a stiff brush and do not attempt to completely cover the characteristics of the wood. Using your finger partially blend the white and black paint. While the paint is still tacky, spread a small amount of powdered metallic color on a sheet of paper and dip the end of one finger into this color. Transfer this color to the driftwood. Blend and highlight as desired. Permit paint to dry and apply one coat of white shellac.

42

DRIFTWOOD,
a little paint,
and a lot of fun

Makes an attractive centerpiece
and a good-looking holder for
potted plants.

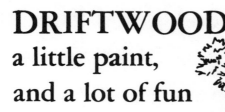

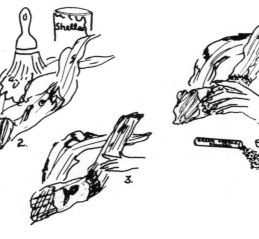

Wire and Raffia Figures

Tools

1. Cutting and slip joint pliers   2. Scissors

Materials and Supplies

1. Wire coat hangers   2. Raffia or crepe paper   3. Rubber cement

Procedure

Using cutting pliers cut a wire coat hanger in the following places: at each end of the straight bottom piece; one side, at the point where the sides join to form the hook. This cutting results in three pieces of wire. Using piece that has the hook on one end, shape to form the body of giraffe. Cut longest remaining piece of wire in half. Each piece is bent in half and placed in the proper place over the body to form the legs. Make one complete turn of each wire around the body and with pliers squeeze tightly in place. Using raffia or narrow strips of crepe paper completely wrap each wire. Ends of paper or raffia may be secured in place by rubber-cementing. In order to provide for additional thickness to appropri-ate portions of the figure, merely wrap with additional layers of raffia or crepe paper.

The mane of the giraffe is constructed by using a 24-inch length of raffia or one-quarter inch strip of crepe paper. Rubber-cement one end of strip on top of head and form one-inch high loop. Using second piece of raffia or one-quarter inch crepe paper strip, wrap loop in place. Continue making loops down neck of giraffe until 24-inch length of raffia or crepe paper is consumed. Eyes can be cut from appropriately colored raffia or crepe paper and glued in place. As in other projects, children should be permitted to select their own designs for figures as well as their own color combinations for these figures.

44

"Put your best figure forward"

... and try this select
treat in the crafts.

*Whisk in and around the
wire in seconds! And see
what your imagination
brings forth.*

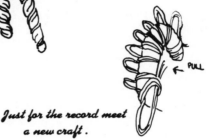

← PULL

*Just for the record meet
a new craft.*

Window shopping for a new craft? Try
this! Combination of wire and raffia!
These adorable animals make ideal decorations and nick-nacks for the childrens'
rooms.

You can hardly call it a party unless one
of these cute figurines has been included.

TRIPLE

DOUBLE

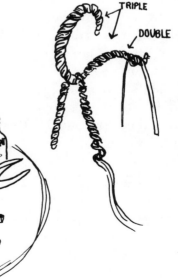

Marbleize-It

Tools

1. Scissors

Materials and Supplies

1. Construction paper or white drawing paper
2. Tray
3. Water
4. Printing ink and turpentine
5. Paper cups or tin cans

Procedure

Pour one-half inch to one inch of water into shallow tray (tray should be at least the size of the paper to be decorated). Place a teaspoon full of printer's ink in a paper cup or tin can. Use as many colors as desired; however, have a separate cup or tin can for each color used. Add four tablespoons of turpentine to each color and mix thoroughly. From each cup pour a small amount of the mixture on the surface of the water. Gently stir surface of water to obtain desired color pattern. Place sheet of paper flat on surface of the fluid. The paper should then be placed, inked side up, on a flat surface to dry. When dry the decorated paper may be used to cover many items, including tin cans, lamp shades, boxes, etc. The paper can be cut to the correct size and rubber-cemented on the object to be decorated.

Discarded jars and bottles can be decorated in the same manner except that oil paint is substituted for printer's ink. The jar or bottle should be thoroughly cleaned and dried. The oil paint of various colors should be thinned with turpentine, and a small amount of these thinned paints is spilled on the surface of the water. Gently rotate a jar or bottle on the surface of the water. This rotating action will pick up the paint and thereby form a colorful and attractive pattern on the surface of the object.

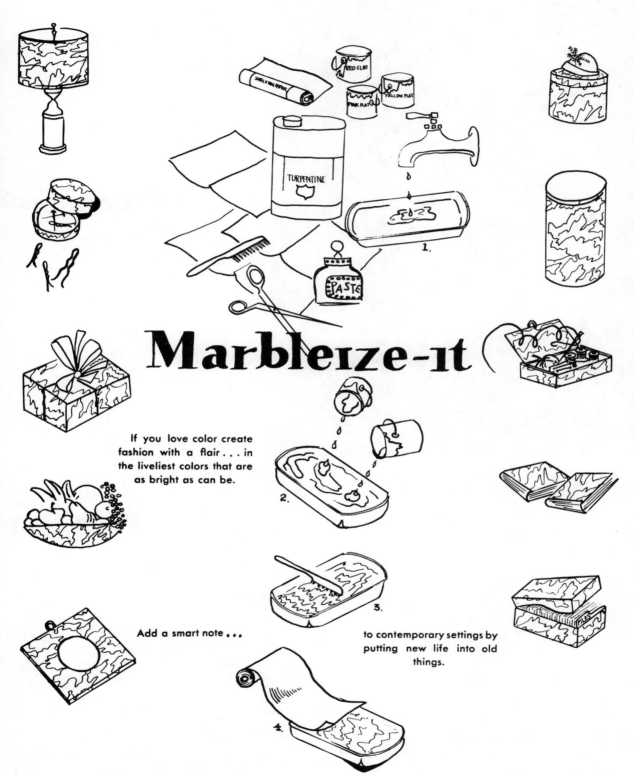

Marbleize-it

If you love color create fashion with a flair . . . in the liveliest colors that are as bright as can be.

Add a smart note . . .

to contemporary settings by putting new life into old things.

1.

2.

3.

4.

Copper Foil Pictures

Tools

1. Pencil with attached eraser
2. Artist's brush
3. Scissors
4. Ruler
5. ½″ brush
6. Hammer
7. Hand saw
8. Fine sandpaper

Materials and Supplies

1. Flat black oil paint
2. 3/0 steel wool
3. Copper foil (36-gauge)
4. Newspaper
5. Masking tape
6. Liver of sulphur
7. Water
8. Clear lacquer
9. ½″ copper escutcheon pins
10. Piece of wood ¼″ x 6″ x 8″

Procedure

With scissors cut a six by eight inch piece of copper foil (do not wrinkle or crease while cutting or handling). Create or select desired design. This beginning design should be principally composed of large mass areas rather than fine detail. (Illustration indicates the type

48

of designs that are appropriate for beginners.) Design should be placed on paper and the paper placed over the piece of copper. Hold paper on copper with masking tape. Place paper covered copper on one-quarter inch thickness of newspaper. Using writing end of pencil, trace lines of design so that the pressure of the point of pencil makes a line in the thin copper. Remove paper from copper and turn copper sheet over on same stack of newspaper. Using the eraser end of pencil push out raised portions of design. Turn copper over and place on hard flat surface. Using eraser end of pencil, flatten background of design.

Very lightly steel-wool entire face of copper. Mix a teaspoon full of liver of sulphur with one pint of water and apply with cloth to copper; permit to dry. Very lightly steel-wool raised portions. Using hand saw cut a piece of one-quarter inch wood six by eight inches; sand the edges. Using escutcheon pins, nail copper around the edges to the cut board, spacing pins approximately one inch apart.

Paint copper picture with clear lacquer. Paint background of picture and edges of one-quarter inch board with flat black paint.

When using copper foil for pins and for earrings press out design in copper as previously described—bend edges of copper over a piece of cardboard that has been cut slightly smaller than the copper. To this cardboard glue with Duco cement as required a pin-back or ear screw. Finish with liver of sulphur and clear lacquer as previously described.

Play it smart and make your own pictures, pins and earrings . . .

it's Ter-rific

This simple process results in beautiful jewelry or decorati e pictures that can be given as gifts.

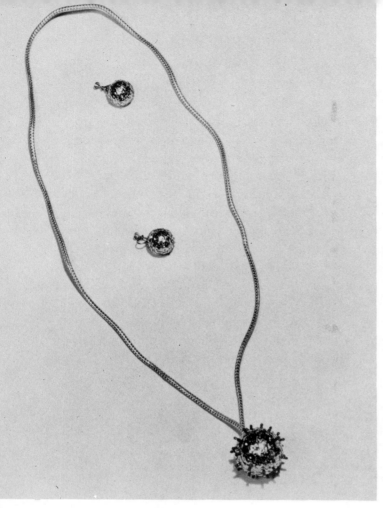

Pendants and Earrings

Tools

1. Awl

Materials and Supplies

1. 1″ spherical corks
2. ⅜″ straight pins (longer ones can be cut down)
3. Sequins
4. Seed beads
5. Ribbon or braided cord
6. Ear backs
7. Duco cement

Procedure

The basic method of construction is the same for both pendants and earrings. The major difference is in the attachment; the pendant requires a ribbon or braided cord, while the earrings require ear backs.

Thread two seed beads on straight pin and pass straight pin through hole in sequin and into cork. Press straight pin into cork until head of pin presses seed beads and sequin tightly against cork. Continue until cork is completely covered with sequins. Space pins evenly in all directions. For pendant remove one pin assembly and in its place force both ends of a 30-inch piece of ribbon or braided cord. With Duco cement fasten ends in place. For earrings use one-half inch diameter corks and decorate as above. Leave out as many pins as necessary to secure ear backs to corks with Duco cement. Be sure to allow sufficient time for cement to set.

A Glittering Delight!

...for mi-lady, on any occasion.
Make a pin, a lavaliere, earrings, or
an entire set.

Smart on a suit or pinned to a hat---
It's the accessories that count.

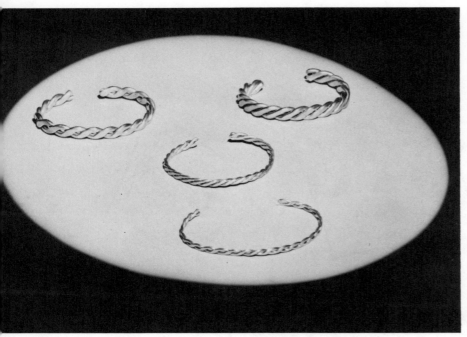

*Twisted
Wire Bracelets*

Tools

1. Cutting pliers
2. Slip joint pliers or hand drill
3. Smooth file

4. Ball peen hammer
5. Artist's brush
6. Small metal plate

Materials and Supplies

1. 3/0 steel wool
2. Clear lacquer

3. 10-gauge soft copper wire and/or 14-gauge copper wire

Procedure

To construct a two-strand twisted wire bracelet use an 18-inch length of 10-gauge copper wire, bend in half; hold both cut ends with pliers or clamp ends in vise. Place bent end in chuck of hand drill, turn hand drill, thereby twisting wires tightly together. If hand drill is not available, twist wires with pair of pliers. Place twisted wires on metal plate and partially flatten with flat face of ball peen hammer. Cut both ends with cutting pliers so that a five-inch piece of twisted flattened wire remains. With

a smooth file round each end and polish with 3/0 steel wool. Bend into shape of bracelet around handle of hammer. Repolish with 3/0 steel wool and paint with clear lacquer, using a clean brush.

To construct three-strand twisted wire bracelet use a 24-inch length of 14-gauge soft copper wire. Bend wire into three equal parts so that each strand is adjacent and parallel to the others. Proceed as indicated for two-strand bracelet.

52

Here's the project that gives you something extra. With a little ingenuity, you can give the original personal touch found in expensive jewelry.

Gifts that are

FUN TO MAKE

and easy, too, if you know the tricks. Make several to take home for your family and friends. Make them for now or to squirrel away for holiday giving.

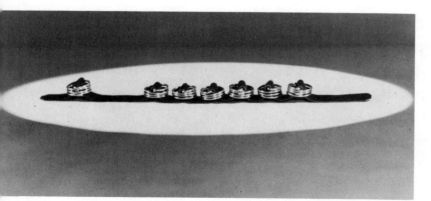

Wire and Leather Bracelets

Tools

1. Coping saw
2. Cutting pliers
3. Ruler
4. Pencil
5. Smooth file
6. Scissors

Materials and Supplies

1. 7 pieces of 14-gauge wire 8″ long
2. Strip of leather or felt ⅝″ x 10″ long
3. ⅝″ dowel 4″ long
4. 3/0 steel wool

Procedure

Using coping saw, cut groove in center of end of dowel. Groove should be one-eighth to one-quarter inch deep and one-sixteenth inch wide. Using cutting pliers cut seven pieces of 14-gauge soft copper wire eight inches long. With smooth file round both ends of each piece of wire, polish with 3/0 steel wool. Place one end of eight-inch length of wire in groove that has been cut in end of five-eighths in dowel. Permit this end to protrude one-eighth inch beyond the dowel. Working from the other end of wire carefully wrap around dowel until wire is consumed. Remove wire form from dowel. Construct six additional forms following the same procedure described above.

From a piece of leather or felt, cut a strip one-half inch wide and ten inches long. With scissors round the two ends of this strip. Pass one end of strip through wire form, over the top of center wire and back down through wire form. Thread the remaining six wire forms on strip in same manner, spacing them one-quarter inch apart. To hold bracelet in place on wrist one end is double threaded through the first wire form.

Our fabulous frauds, copied from extravagant jewelry, are genuine flattery. Necklaces, chokers, and centered ornaments! All can have matching bracelets! What glamourous gifts, and exclusively yours.

Natural beauty reflects dramatic design and warm color combinations — graceful design makes this an unusual project idea.

The Benefit of No Doubt!

For those who demand the best, this project is worth mentioning. Add a smart note to your wardrobe, with these fashionable sets.

1.

←WIRE

2.

3.

4.

5.

6.

Rhythm Drums

Tools

1. Can Opener
2. Leather punch
3. ½″ paint brush
4. Scissors

Materials and Supplies

1. Empty #10 tin can
2. Discarded automobile inner tube or piece of leather
3. Oil paints or construction paper and rubber cement
4. Round plastic lacing

Procedure

Obtain an empty #10 tin can from a local restaurant or cafeteria. Completely remove both ends of can with can opener. (Use type of can opener that does not leave a ragged edge or sharp burr on inside of can.) Wash resultant cylinder in water and remove paper labels; wipe dry.

Outside surface of metal cylinder may be decorated by painting or covering with colored paper. If cylinder is to be painted use quick drying oil-based paints, and apply in desired pattern. If colored paper is to be used join paper to surface of cylinder with rubber cement.

Obtain discarded automobile inner tube from a local garage. Place inner tube flat on table and with a pair of scissors cut completely around inside diameter of tube. Open tube to form a single thickness of rubber. Place end of cylinder on top of rubber sheeting. With a pencil draw a circle on the rubber sheeting— two inches larger in radius than the circle formed by end of cylinder. Cut out circle with scissors. Using a ruler draw four diameters that will divide the circle into eight approximately equal parts. Where each diameter intersects the circumference of the circle measure in three-quarters of an inch. On this imaginary circle punch one-eighth inch holes one-half inch to each side of the four diameters. A total of sixteen holes are punched. Construct from the rubber sheeting a second drum head.

Center a drum head on each end of cylinder. Using a ten-foot length of round plastic lacing pass one end through punched hole of either drum head and through hole in opposite drum head. Draw drum heads tight and knot ends of lacing together. Wrap with plastic lacing drum head to cylinder. This wrapping should be composed of at least six turns of lacing and should be placed as close to the ends of the cylinder as possible. Drum heads may be decorated by painting with oil paints. If leather is used for drum heads the same procedure is used to construct the drum, except that the leather is soaked in water prior to lacing in place. The leather is then permitted to dry out before using the drum.

The drum beater is constructed using a one-quarter inch dowel; with a knife cut a groove one inch from one end. A wad of cotton or cloth is wrapped around the end of the dowel that has been grooved. A piece of rubber is stretched over the wrapped cotton or cloth and held in place by binding with plastic lacing. Binding should be placed over groove in dowel to prevent wrapping from slipping off the one-quarter inch dowel handle.

rhythm drums

Odds 'n' ends
go into these attractive playthings.
Only a few tools needed, So roll up
your sleeves and let's get started on
our own rhythm band.

Bark Houses

Tools

1. Knife
2. Ruler
3. Scissors
4. Pencil
5. ½" brush

Materials and Supplies

1. Cedar or birch bark
2. Twigs
3. Cellophane
4. Flat toothpicks
5. Rubber cement
6. Masking tape
7. Cardboard
8. Fine sandpaper
9. Duco cement

Procedure

This unusual project idea provides ample opportunity for youngsters to design and construct a scale model home, cabin, or building of their own choice. The basic method of construction is identical regardless of the type of building selected.

The basic design is drawn on paper. From this drawing measurements are taken of the four sides of the house and these dimensions are transferred to cardboard. Windows and doors are placed in the appropriate locations on the cardboard. Windows are completely cut out while the doors are cut only on the top and one side (the bottom side is one end of the cardboard and the uncut side of door pro-

vides the hinge). The four walls are placed on top of a piece of cardboard and with masking tape they are held in position. The roof is likewise constructed of cardboard and also held in place with masking tape. Coat the entire wall and roof surfaces of house with thin coat of rubber cement. Cut to length, as required, strips of cedar or birch bark. Coat the inner side of these strips with rubber cement and permit to dry. When dry place on sides and roof of house. Carefully fit these strips to resemble a log cabin. The chimney is also constructed of cardboard and may be covered with fine sandpaper that is cemented over the cardboard. Lines should be drawn on rough surface of sandpaper to resemble the joints between stones. Windows are made of Cellophane and toothpicks. Outside posts to support porch roof are cut from twigs and glued into place, using Duco cement. Overlapping strips of construction paper could be used in place of cedar bark. These strips would give the appearance of siding or shingles. Red construction paper could be lined with pencil and ruler to resemble red brick and cemented to the sides of the house. For the smaller children a cardboard cracker box could be used to provide a beginning structure upon which to build.

Cardboard,
twigs, bark, and glue
add

up to this —
Design it for its
use, and use it
as you wish —

Wire Figures

Tools

1. Cutting pliers
2. Hammer

Materials and Supplies

1. ¼" plywood 2" x 2"
2. 1" brad
3. Duco cement
4. 12 ft. cotton covered 24-gauge soft wire

Procedure

Cut four pieces of 24-gauge cotton covered wire four and one-half inches long and place in a bundle. To form the chest and arms start at the center of a 36-inch piece of wire, wrap one end slightly above the center and towards one end of the four and one-half inch bundle. Make eight complete turns. Using the second end of the 36-inch piece of wire, wrap in the same direction and on top of the first, wrapping eight complete turns. From the four and one-half inch bundle bend two lengths of wire at right angles and opposite one another. With the two ends of wire used to wrap the body, continue with these ends to wrap the arms. Make sixteen turns to complete each arm. Cut off the surplus wire.

To form the hips and legs, use a second piece of 24-gauge cotton covered wire 36 inches long. Starting in the center of this piece and directly under the chest, wrap four turns toward the legs. Using the second end of the 36-inch piece of wire, wrap four turns in the same direction and on top of the first wrapping. Split ends of bundle that stick out of the wrapping into two pairs of wires. These wires will form the base for the leg wrappings. Continue with one end of the wrapping down each leg, making 24 complete turns to form each leg. Permit center wire of each leg to stick out one-quarter inch and cut off. Bend at right angles to leg in order to form the foot. Cut off any surplus wrapping.

To form the head use six inches of the 24-gauge cotton covered wire. Starting in the center of this wire and using one end, start from the shoulders and wrap the two remaining wires with four to six turns. Using the second end of the eight inch piece, wrap four to six turns in the same direction and on top of the first wrapping. Cut off surplus ends.

To form the base, use 48 inches of 24-gauge cotton covered wire. Drive a brad through center of the plywood and make a small hole next to the driven nail. Put one end of the wire into the hole and wrap flat layer of wire around the nail and flat on the plywood. Continue wrapping until 48-inch length of wire is consumed. Spread a thin coat of Duco cement on top of the wrapped wire; permit this to dry and remove from the plywood. Glue the feet to the wrapped base with Duco cement and permit to dry.

To form the drum, use a 12-inch length of 24-gauge cotton covered wire. Start from one end of wire and make eight turns around a three-eighths inch dowel or pencil. Remove the wire from the dowel or pencil. Bend and cement long end to inside of drum; hang over neck of figure. Shape and bend figure as desired. When wrapping long lengths of wire make small loop on loose ends to insure safe handling.

Give it a
BRAND-NEW TWIST

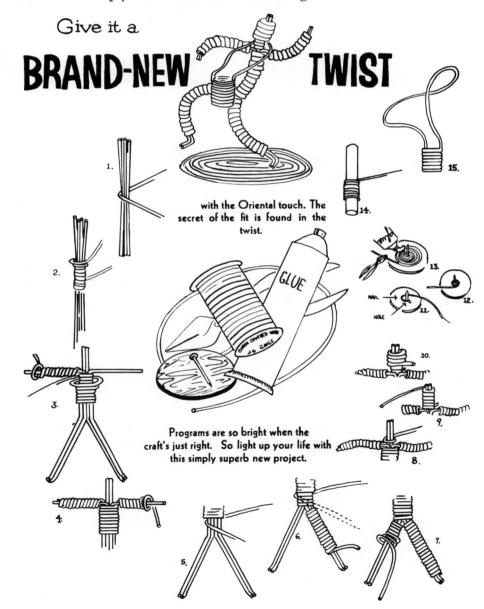

with the Oriental touch. The secret of the fit is found in the twist.

Programs are so bright when the craft's just right. So light up your life with this simply superb new project.

Kites

Tools

1. Coping saw
2. Pencil
3. Ruler

4. Scissors
5. Artist's brush

Materials and Supplies

1. 1 stick approximately $\frac{3}{16}''$ x $\frac{1}{4}''$ x 36"
2. 1 stick approximately $\frac{3}{16}''$ x $\frac{1}{4}''$ x 24"
3. String
4. Rubber cement

5. Tissue paper or thin wrapping paper
6. Tempera paints
7. Cloth

Procedure

Obtain two three-sixteenths by one-quarter inch sticks from scrap pile in local lumber yard.

One stick should be cut 24 inches long and the other 36 inches long. Using coping saw cut a shallow groove in both ends of each stick. This groove should be cut in the center of the ends of the sticks so that the saw cut runs parallel to the one-quarter inch face. Measure 12 inches from one end of the larger stick. Place the mid point of the short stick directly over this mark so that the sticks form a cross. (Make certain that the one-quarter inch faces of the sticks are in contact with each other.) At the point of intersection bind the two sticks together with string. Place a continuous string in grooves that have been cut in ends of sticks and draw string tight, but do not distort sticks. Tie ends of string together and cut off loose ends. Place kite form on top of tissue paper or thin wrapping paper. Paper should be at least 26 inches wide and 38 inches long. (If a large single sheet of paper is not available several smaller sheets can be combined and held together with rubber cement.) With pencil, sketch a line on the paper that is one inch larger on all four sides of the kite frame; as outlined by the connecting string. Fold com-

pletely around the kite the one inch extra tab of paper over the string and back over itself; rubber-cement in place. Tie a length of string to one end of the 24-inch stick. Bring string across the back of the kite to the other end of the 24-inch stick and gently draw string tight until a "belly" develops on the back of the kite; fasten string. (A distance of four inches should be observed at the center of the kite between the taut string and the 24-inch stick.)

Measure in eight inches from each end of the 36-inch stick. At these points make a small hole through the paper on each side of the stick. Through the top set of holes and around the stick attach one end of a 28-inch length of string. Attach other end of string to bottom half of stick. String should be loose. Knot kite cord to this string so that knot can slide on string when slight pressure is applied. For kite tail, tear small pieces of cloth and attach these pieces together with a single length of string. (The greater the wind, the longer the tail should be.) Attach string to bottom of kite.

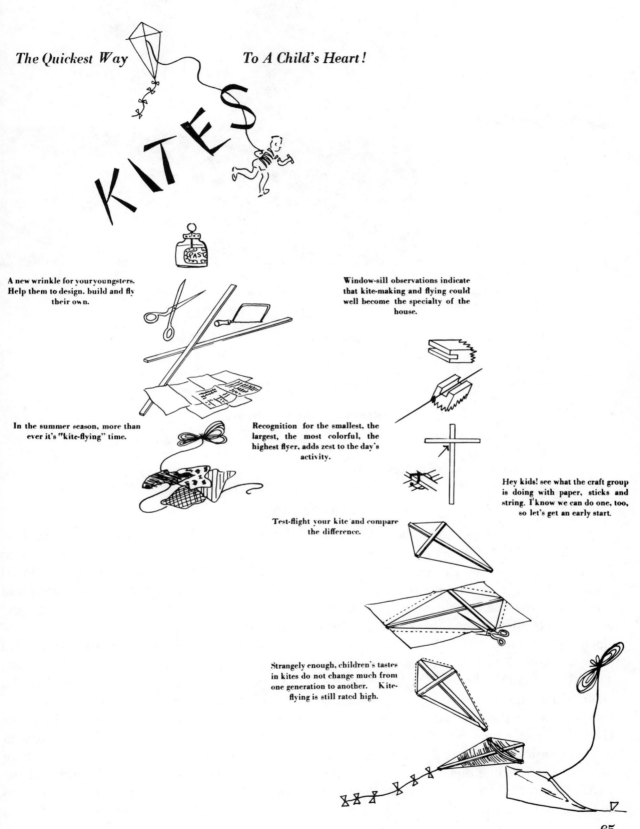

The Quickest Way   *To A Child's Heart!*

KITES

A new wrinkle for your youngsters. Help them to design. build and fly their own.

Window-sill observations indicate that kite-making and flying could well become the specialty of the house.

In the summer season, more than ever it's "kite-flying" time.

Recognition for the smallest, the largest, the most colorful, the highest flyer, adds zest to the day's activity.

Hey kids! see what the craft group is doing with paper, sticks and string. I know we can do one, too, so let's get an early start.

Test-flight your kite and compare the difference.

Strangely enough, children's tastes in kites do not change much from one generation to another. Kite-flying is still rated high.

Sailboats

Tools

1. Coping saw
2. Hand drill
3. ¼" twist drill
4. Hammer
5. Halfround file
6. C-clamp
7. Paint brush
8. Pencil
9. Ruler
10. Knife
11. Scissors

Materials and Supplies

1. Wood
2. ¼" dowel
3. Heavy waxpaper or construction paper
4. Paints
5. Duco cement
6. Sandpaper
7. Brads

Procedure

Obtain a piece of lumber three-quarters or one inch thick (end of an orange crate will do). Draw a rectangle four by ten inches on the board, making certain that the ten-inch dimension is with the grain of the wood. From one end of rectangle measure back three inches along the ten-inch sides. From these points draw a line to the center of the nearest end. These lines form the bow of the boat. On the other end of the rectangle (the stern of the boat) draw two small arcs at the corners. Using C-clamp, clamp board to table and cut out boat with coping saw; file and sandpaper smooth. Draw a line down the center of the boat. Measure three inches from the bow and one and one-half inch from the stern on the center line; drill a one-quarter inch hole one-half inch deep at these two points. Using Duco cement glue a one-quarter inch dowel ten inches long in each hole. For cabin add blocks of wood and nail in place. Paint and decorate as desired.

To construct sail use heavy wax paper (will not spoil by wetting) or construction paper. Cut two rectangles four by six inches. In the center of the six-inch sides and one inch in from each of the sides, cut a slit in the paper one-half inch long and parallel to the six-inch sides. Place one sail over each of the masts so that the dowel goes through the slits and the sail curves toward the stern of the boat to provide a realistic appearance.

SAIL BOATS

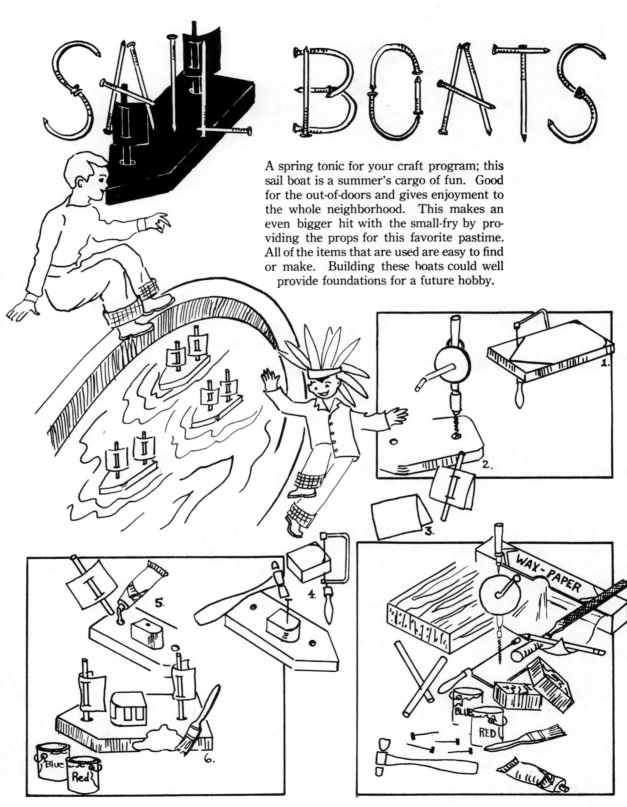

A spring tonic for your craft program; this sail boat is a summer's cargo of fun. Good for the out-of-doors and gives enjoyment to the whole neighborhood. This makes an even bigger hit with the small-fry by providing the props for this favorite pastime. All of the items that are used are easy to find or make. Building these boats could well provide foundations for a future hobby.

1.

2.

3.

4.

5.

6.

WAY - PAPER

Blue

Red

Blue

Red

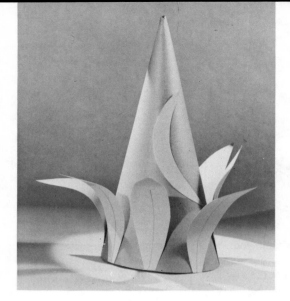

Party Hats

Tools

1. Scissors
2. Compass
3. Pencil
4. Ruler
5. Artist's brush

Materials and Supplies

1. Construction paper
2. Rubber cement
3. Tempera paint

Procedure

The illustration shows two basic forms that may be employed in the construction of party hats. The first form is a cylinder, while the second is a cone.

For the cylindrical hat use a strip of paper to measure the circumference of the youngster's head at the point where the hat is to fit. Add one-half inch to this measurement; determine the height of the hat. On a piece of construction paper lay out the rectangle desired. Assuming the hat is to be 12 inches high and 18 inches in circumference, bring the short ends of the paper together and overlap one-half inch and cement with rubber cement. On one end of the cylinder cut a series of V-cuts to a depth of three-quarters of an inch and bend in the tabs toward the center of the cylinder.

Measure the diameter of the cylinder and with a compass construct a circle on construction paper. Cut the circle out with scissors and rubber-cement to the tabs on top of the hat. Design bill of hat and cut out of construction paper. Cut a series of V's in the bill at the point of attachment to body of hat, and rubber-cement the tabs of bill to body of hat. Cement small piece of construction paper over V's of the bill. Paint or decorate as desired.

For the cone shaped hat, construct a 15-inch square on construction paper. With a compass, or a piece of string attached to a pencil, and using one corner of the square as the center of the arc, construct an arc that intersects the adjacent corners of the square. Cut out with scissors. Using the larger of the two pieces of construction paper, overlap and join with rubber cement the straight sides of the paper. Test the cone for size. Cut in the form of leaves pieces of construction paper and cement these to the hat. Additional decoration employing tempera paint and construction paper may be used, taking into consideration the intent and purpose of the hat.

Jiffy Party hats

Quick start for festive programs. Cook up the latest "Paris Fashions" with these jiffy hats.

Spruce up your program by crowning the king and queen of your party.

Tools

1. Coping saw
2. Artist's brush
3. Pencil
4. Ruler

5. Compass
6. ¼″ twist drill
7. Staple gun or hammer

Materials and Supplies

1. Piece of ¼″ plywood 6″ x 8″
2. Piece of ¼″ plywood 2½″ x 2½″
3. Oil paint

4. Carbon and construction paper
5. Fine sandpaper
6. Staple or ¾″ brad

Procedure

Construct a six by eight inch rectangle on piece of construction paper. Starting from one side of rectangle draw a series of parallel lines one-half inch apart to opposite side. Working from adjacent side of rectangle draw a series of lines one-half inch apart to other end. The six by eight inch rectangle should now be filled with one-half inch squares created by the intersecting pencil lines.

Transfer the points of intersection from the illustration to the appropriate locations on your six by eight inch rectangle. Using a pencil connect these points. The resultant drawing should be twice the size of the illustration. Using pencil, fill in features and hair as desired. Transfer design with carbon paper to plywood. With a coping saw cut out along exterior lines and smooth edges with fine sandpaper. Paint as desired.

For the ring, construct a two and one-half inch circle on one-quarter inch plywood. Construct a one and three-quarter inch circle concentric to the first. Drill a one-quarter inch hole through one and three-quarter inch circle, and insert coping saw blade in hole; attach coping saw frame to blade and cut out the one and three-quarter inch circle. Remove blade from hole and cut out two and one-half inch circle. Smooth edges of ring and attach one end of a three-foot string to edge of ring, using staple gun or small brad. Attach in same manner other end of string to edge of chin or end of nose. Paint plywood ring as desired, using oil base paint.

70

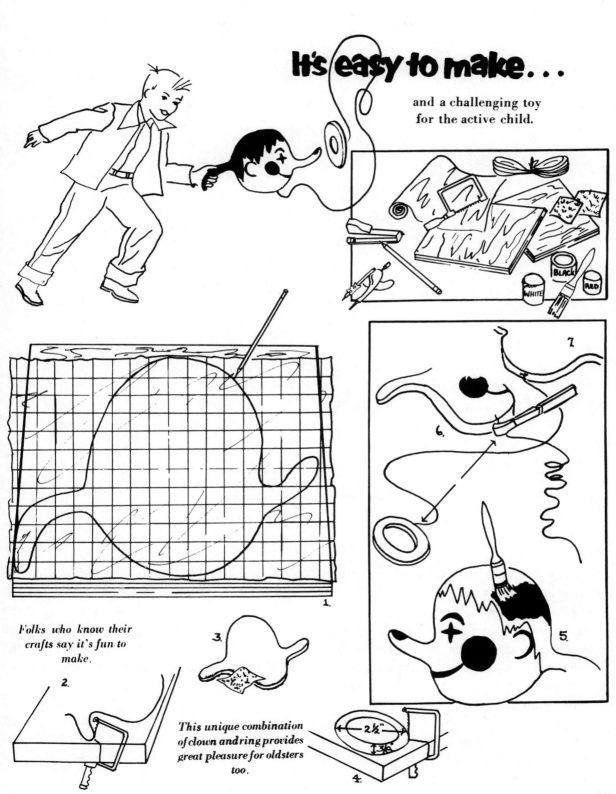

It's easy to make...

and a challenging toy for the active child.

Folks who know their crafts say it's fun to make.

This unique combination of clown and ring provides great pleasure for oldsters too.

BLACK

WHITE

RED

1.

2.

3.

4.

2½"

1 3/8"

5.

6.

7.

Mobile

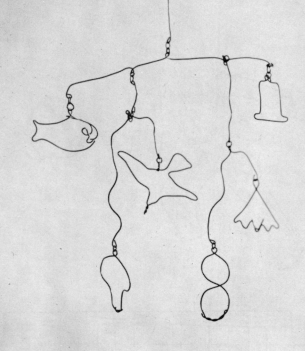

1. Cutting pliers   2. Slip joint pliers or long nose pliers

Materials and Supplies

1. 18-gauge copper wire

Procedure

The basic concept to remember in the construction of a mobile is balance. Delicate balance is necessary in order that even the slightest movement of air against the component parts will keep the mobile in constant motion. The illustration indicates a mobile constructed from 18-gauge copper wire. The basic design for each component part is an angel fish. However, each unit is of different size. It is suggested that a full size paper drawing be made of the desired mobile; include in this drawing the actual size of each component part. This

drawing may then be used as a ready reference when bending and forming your wire to develop the desired shape for each unit. Start with a single hook to hang mobile. This hook is loosely fastened to a horizontal piece of wire. (To provide adequate support, heavier and larger mobiles require thicker and stiffer wire.) After this point one can plan, develop, and balance the unit as desired. Other materials, forms, etc., may also be incorporated in the basic idea in order to match existing motifs, forms, and patterns.

Make·them·
RAVE

Nipple Dolls

Tools

1. Scissors
2. Artist's brush or sewing needle
3. Pencil
4. Ruler
5. Compass

Materials and Supplies

1. Nipple from baby bottle
2. Crepe paper or fabric
3. Tempera paints
4. Rubber cement (if crepe paper is used)
5. Thread (if fabric is used)
6. Shellac

Procedure

Obtain a rubber nipple from a baby bottle; using tempera paint, paint features on bulb end. When dry, coat with shellac. On crepe paper or cloth construct a 12-inch circle. Inside this circle and concentric to it construct a two inch circle. Using the radius of the larger circle (six inches), divide the circumference of the larger circle into six equal parts. From these points draw straight lines to the center of the circle. With scissors cut out the following: the two-inch circle, discard; the 12-inch circle and two adjacent segments. The remaining larger piece is joined at the straight sides with needle and thread if fabric is used, or rubber cement if crepe paper is employed. Into the top of this truncated cone the rubber nipple is placed and rubber-cemented. A hat is designed and cut from fabric or crepe paper and cemented in place. A large bow at the neck is likewise designed and placed in position to cover the joint between the nipple and dress. The fabric or crepe paper is decorated as desired.

In the illustration showing the development of dress, the dotted line indicates a method whereby guide lines for future designs can be drawn.

74

A Cute Stunt

12"

6"

2 3/8"

Shellac

RED

RUBBER CEMENT

BLUE

CREPE PAPER

Bracelets

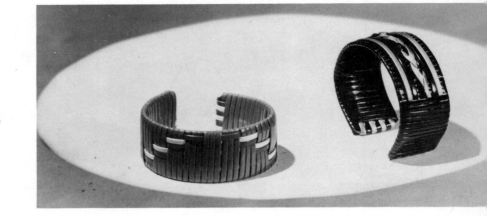

Tools

1. Ruler
2. Tin snips
3. 6″ smooth file
4. Scratch awl

Materials and Supplies

1. 5⁄8″ x 6″ metal banding (or 24-gauge sheet metal)
2. 7 strips of 3⁄32″ plastic lacing 10″ long (colors as desired)
3. 1 strip 3⁄32″ plastic lacing 3 yards long
4. 6″ strip of Scotch tape

Procedure

Using tin snips cut a six-inch strip of metal banding; with a file slightly round each of the four corners. Place the seven ten-inch strips of lacing flat, parallel, and lengthwise on the metal strip, allowing two inches of each strip to extend over each end of the metal. Bend all ends of the lacing over the ends of metal and fasten these ends with masking tape to back of metal strip.

At one end of the bracelet slide one end of a three-yard piece of lacing between the lacing and back of metal strip. This end should merely extend to one edge of the bracelet. Using the other end of the three-yard piece of lacing and working from the end and towards the center of the bracelet, wrap five parallel turns of lac-

ing. Loosen the three center strips of lacing from other end and flat braid these three strips to end of metal banding.

Temporarily fasten the ends of the braid with Scotch tape. Holding the braided strip perpendicular to the metal, continue to wrap bracelet with long end of lacing to within one-half inch of other end of bracelet. Remove masking tape and place braided strip flat along center of bracelet, and bend over end of metal banding and fasten to back with Scotch tape. Continue wrapping bracelet to end of metal banding. Slide end of lacing between metal and lacing; cut off excess lacing and long ends on back. Bend to desired shape over wrist or dowel.

Gifts-To-Make

A few colorful materials,
plus skill and imagination—and
you're ready to try your hand at this

BACK

LACING

Scotch Tape

1.

2.

3.

4.

5.

6.

7.

Casting Arrows

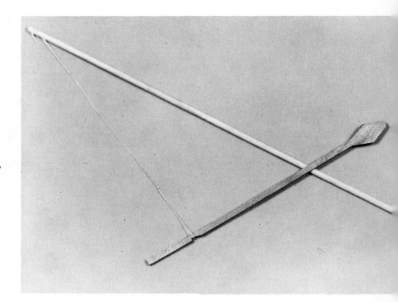

Tools

1. Ruler
2. Pencil
3. Coping saw
4. C-clamp
5. Artist's brush (if desired)
6. Scissors

Materials and Supplies

1. 18" wooden shingle
2. ½" dowel or stick 3' long
3. String
4. Fine sandpaper
5. Paints (if desired)
6. Construction paper

Procedure

To construct pattern for arrows use construction paper. Draw two parallel lines three-eighths inch apart and 18 inches long. From same ends of each line measure in three-quarters inch and two inches. Perpendicular to each line at the three-quarter inch mark measure out three-quarters inch. On each side connect this point with end of arrow and two-inch mark. With scissors cut out pattern. Place pattern on 18 inch wooden shingle so that widest part of arrow is over the thin end of shingle. Clamp thin end of shingle to table and with coping saw first cut out thick part of arrow.

(Cutting the thick part of arrow at beginning will provide maximum support when cutting out thin end of arrow.) Cut out remaining portion of arrow. Lightly sandpaper and place over one finger to determine center of balance. From this point measure one-quarter inch towards the thick end of arrow. On side of arrow construct a groove to hold string (*see* illustration). Paint or decorate. Using a 30-inch length of string, make a three-inch loop in one end and attach other end to end of a three-foot dowel or stick. Place loop in groove of arrow. Cast arrow as one casts a fishing line.

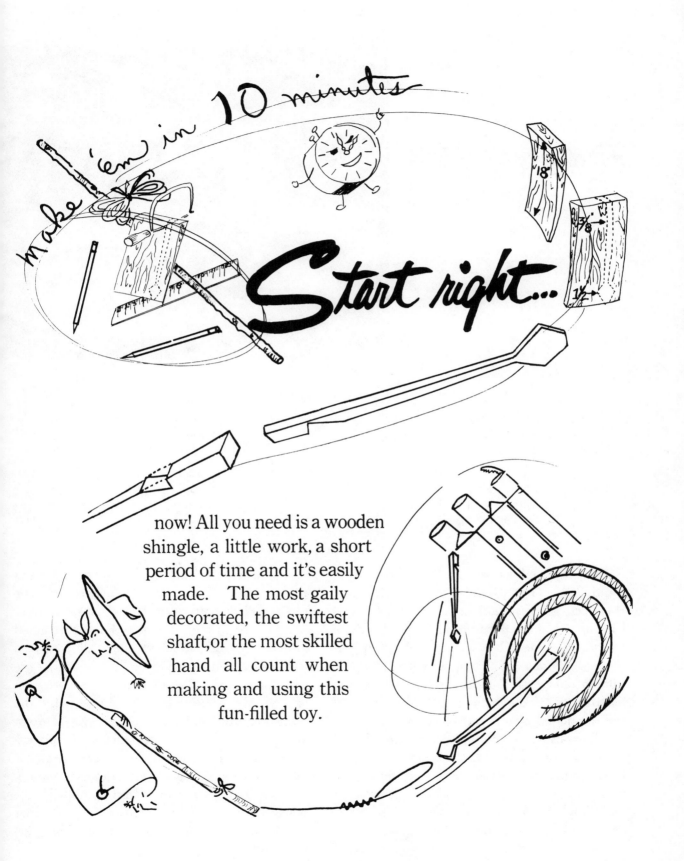

make 'em in 10 minutes

Start right...

now! All you need is a wooden shingle, a little work, a short period of time and it's easily made. The most gaily decorated, the swiftest shaft, or the most skilled hand all count when making and using this fun-filled toy.

Pedigreed Pets

Tools

1. Scissors
2. Sewing needle

3. Ruler
4. Pencil

Materials and Supplies

1. Felt or fabric
2. Buttons
3. Sewing thread

4. Round toothpicks
5. Graph paper

Procedure

The patterns illustrated on the page opposite could well be used to construct this stuffed toy. However, the resultant mouse would be one-half the size of the illustration. To employ these patterns use one-half or one-inch graph paper. If one-half inch graph paper is used, the resultant mouse will be the same size as the illustration. If one-inch graph paper is used the completed mouse will be twice the size of the illustration. In either case the method used to develop the patterns is the same. Locate the intersecting points formed by the outline of the individual pattern pieces and the one-quarter inch graph lines. Transfer these points to the corresponding places on the large graph paper. Connect these lines. Cut out pattern. Illustra-

tion indicates the number of individual pattern pieces that are required for each part of the mouse. Place patterns on felt or fabric and cut out. Each part of the mouse is constructed individually and attached when all parts are completed. The parts are: body, head, ears, arms, legs, tail. The method of construction is the same for all units. Merely assemble the pieces required and sew together as illustrated. When the sewing of a unit is almost completed, stuff with cotton and finish sewing. Assemble units and carefully sew together to form mouse. Sew on buttons for eyes and toothpicks for whiskers. Use your imagination for any other additions, taking into consideration the purpose and use of your pedigreed pet.

80

Pedigreed Pets

You need

- Scissors ☑
- Sewing Needle ☑
- Ruler ☑
- Pencil ☑
- Felt or Fabric ☑
- Buttons ☑
- Sewing thread ☑
- Round toothpicks ☑
- Graph paper ☑

OUT OF NURSERY RHYMES
GREW THIS LOVABLE PET
OF FANTASY LAND. THIS
MOUSE IS IDEAL FOR SMALL
PRIVATE COLLECTIONS,
AND WHAT'S MORE, FABRICS
CAN COME FROM THE SCRAP
BASKET

Pedigreed
Pets

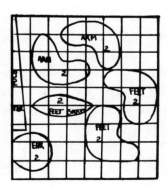

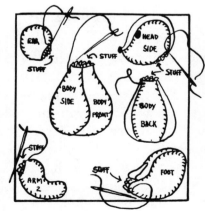

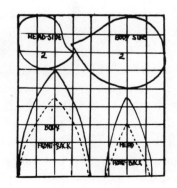

Spool Marionettes

Tools

1. Ruler
2. Scissors
3. Sewing needle
4. Pencil
5. Compass

Materials and Supplies

1. 3 empty sewing thread spools 1⅜" in diameter by 1¾" long
2. 4 empty sewing thread spools 1" in diameter by 1⅜" long
3. Sewing thread #40
4. Cotton padding
5. Heavy cloth or light felt
6. Drawing paper
7. Straight pins
8. Table tennis ball
9. Soft wire

Procedure

To develop pattern for body and legs cut a six by seven inch rectangle out of drawing paper. Measure in two inches from each of the four corners of the rectangle along the seven-inch sides. From these points draw a line perpendicular to the seven-inch sides and in one and three-quarters inches. Connect the ends of these lines that are on the same sides of the rectangle. Cut out both small rectangles. The remaining pattern now looks like a crude box letter "H". Place pattern on cloth and hold in place with straight pins; cut out with scissors.

Cut out second piece of material, using same pattern. Place material on top of one another with good sides of fabric against one another. Using needle and thread sew all edges together with the following exceptions: at the ends of each leg; where head joins body leave a two-inch section open to provide for the insertion of the spools. Turn fabric right side out.

Place spools in position and tie as illustrated. When trying leave one inch between small spools and large spools, and one-half inch between large spools. Through opening at the neck insert spool assembly and place in proper positions. For the pads of the feet cut four circles one and three-eighths inches in diameter. Lightly pad end of spools that form legs with cotton padding and place one and three-eighths inch circle of cloth over padding and sew to leg. For head cut a four-inch circle of fabric and stretch over table tennis ball. Sew in place. Place gathered fabric ends of head in side of body at neck and sew head to body. Sew or glue in place pieces of fabric representing ears, eyes, nose, etc. For the tail cut a triangle from fabric where adjacent sides are four inches long and where base is three-quarters inch wide; sew long sides of fabric together and insert a piece of wire to stiffen. Sew tail in place. Attach control threads to places indicated on drawing.

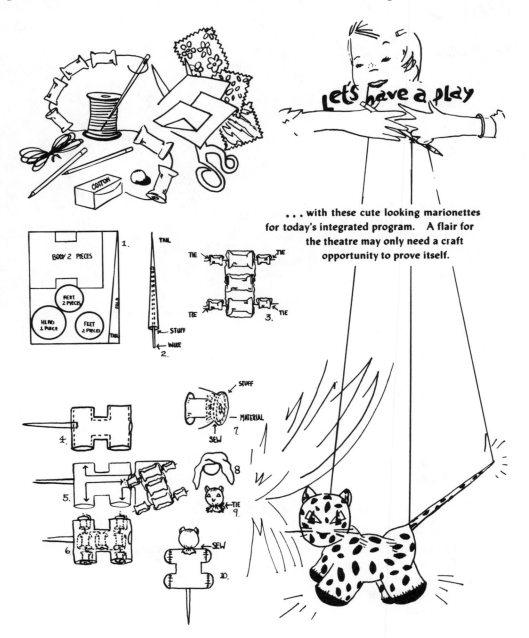

Let's have a play

. . . with these cute looking marionettes for today's integrated program. A flair for the theatre may only need a craft opportunity to prove itself.

83

Plaster of Paris Lamp

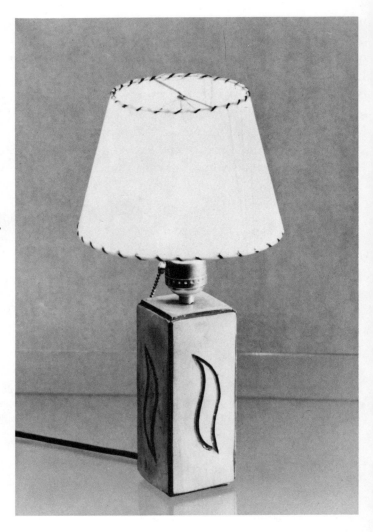

Tools

1. Screw driver
2. Knife
3. ½" brush
4. Artist's brush

Materials and Supplies

1. 1-quart milk container
2. ⅜" dowel 12" long
3. Grease or Vaseline
4. Small piece of felt
5. Rubber cement
6. Lamp wire
7. Lamp socket and plug
8. Fine sandpaper
9. Shellac
10. Mixing container
11. Plaster of Paris
12. Water
13. 2" length of ⅛" pipe
14. Tempera paint
15. Duco cement

Procedure

Cut a three-eighths inch hole in the center of the top of a quart milk container. Grease a three-eighths dowel and push dowel through hole until the end of the dowel strikes the center of the bottom of milk container.

Pour one quart of water into the mixing pail; slowly add plaster of Paris until the water no longer absorbs the plaster of Paris; stir mixture. Fill milk container with mixture, making certain that the dowel remains upright and centered in the milk container. Gently tap sides of container to remove air bubbles. When the container becomes warm, remove the dowel and carefully tear the milk container from the solid form of plaster. Using a knife, slightly round the square corners and smooth with fine sandpaper. A design may be cut in the sides of the plaster form. Paint, using tempera paint, and permit to dry. Apply a thin coat of shellac, brushing with long, even strokes (avoid over-brushing as the colors will run together).

In a clockwise direction, carefully turn a two-inch length of one-eighth inch threaded pipe into the hole on the top of the plaster form. Permit pipe to extend three-eighths inch above the top of the plaster form. Push one end of the lamp wire through the pipe and out the bottom of the plaster form, allowing two inches of the wire to protrude from the pipe. Using a knife, cut a groove in the bottom of the plaster form from the center hole to one side of the form. Place the wire in the groove and rubber-cement a small piece of felt over the bottom of the plaster form. Screw socket base on one-eighth pipe. Remove one-half inch insulation from both ends of wire. Attach socket and plug to appropriate ends of wire. Test before using.

If you love color and startling design. . .

WANT TO DECORATE?

Something worth showing after you're through. Strikingly effective with our casual mode of living, this lamp provides that certain something. So easy to make with a few tools and comparatively little work.

Brushes

Tools

1. Scissors

Materials and Supplies

1. Rainbow fibre (or substitute)
2. Masking tape
3. Round plastic lacing

Procedure

Obtain a bundle of rainbow fiber or fine grass that is ten inches long and approximately three-quarters to one inch in diameter. From this bundle remove an amount equal in diameter to that of a pencil. With one-half inch wide masking tape, tape one end of small bundle; two turns of tape will be sufficient. (When using masking tape throughout this project, be certain that each layer of tape is placed directly over the preceding layer.) Working from the taped end divide this bundle into three equal parts and braid entire length. Fasten second end with masking tape. Trim all loose fibres with scissors. Bring taped ends of braided piece together and overlap one-half inch; tape together to form a ring. Pass remaining bundle of fibres half way through this ring and bend over joint of braided ring. Tightly bind the fibres with masking tape. Binding should be placed close to ring (see illustration). Over this tape wrap a layer of round plastic lacing. The most effective way to accomplish this wrapping is to use a 36-inch piece of round plastic lacing. Make a three inch loop at one of the ends of the 36-inch length of lacing. Place this loop against and parallel to the brush section. The loop end should be facing the handle of the brush. Start wrapping with long

87

end of lacing *towards* the loop end, and around the fibre and the loop end of the lacing. When length of lacing is consumed, place end into loop and pull other end of 36-inch length of lacing until both ends are crossed underneath and in the middle of the wrapped area. Trim lacing and fibres. Fan out ends of brush and trim them again.

Something new!

Dust your jacket,
dust your skirt,
brush it clean and
hang this small broom near;
for a very handy accessory.

88

Skate Scooter

Tools

1. Hand saw
2. Hammer
3. Ruler
4. Pencil
5. 1″ paint brush
6. ½″ round file

Materials and Supplies

1. Paint
2. 6-penny common nails
3. 1 piece of 2″ x 3″ x 36″ lumber
4. Discarded wooden box
5. 2 pieces of 1″ x 2″ x 18″ lumber
6. 1 roller skate

Procedure

From one roller skate remove the two bolts that hold front wheel assembly to rear assembly and separate. Remove front clamp. Cut a piece of two by three inch lumber 36 inches long. To each end of this board fasten with nails one wheel assembly of separated roller skate. Nail one end of box to end of 36-inch board. Make certain that 36-inch board is centered on the end of the box and that the bottom of box is flush with end of 36-inch board. Place two one by two by 18-inch strips of wood on top end of box to form handles. Nail handles to box in desired position. File and sandpaper handles to desired shape. Paint and decorate scooter as desired, employing oil paint if scooter is to be used out-of-doors.

Linoleum Block Prints

Tools

1. Linoleum cutting tools or X-acto knife or even single-edge razor blade
2. Brayer
3. Pencil

Materials and Supplies

1. Drawing or construction paper
2. Piece Battleship linoleum
3. Linoleum block ink or printer's ink
4. Glass plate
5. Carbon paper
6. Masking tape
7. Tracing paper
8. Wiping cloth

Procedure

Create desired design on drawing paper. Beginners should select a simple design. This design should be devoid of fine detail. Place piece of tracing paper over design and trace. Place carbon paper (use white carbon paper on dark linoleum) face down on top of smooth side of linoleum. Place tracing paper *face down* (design will be reversed if placed face up) on top of carbon paper and with pencil transfer lines to linoleum. Using linoleum cutting tools, X-acto knife, or even a single-edge razor blade, cut out to an approximate depth of one-sixteenth of an inch those areas of the design in the linoleum that, in order to form the design, should be removed.

Place a small amount of linoleum block printing ink on a piece of glass and with brayer, roll out ink on glass (use only enough ink to form a thin film on glass). Transfer ink to linoleum by rolling brayer on cut surface of linoleum. Move brayer in all directions in order to obtain a uniform film of ink on raised portions of design. Place sheet of drawing or construction paper on inked surface of linoleum. Clean ink from brayer and roll brayer over paper. This rolling action of brayer forces paper against raised portions of design, thereby transferring ink to paper. Check accuracy of cutting by observing print. Make adjustments as needed.

A wash wringer may be used as a substitute for the brayer when printing. Merely insert inked linoleum in center of magazine with sheet of paper over the inked surface and press in wash wringer. Avoid excessive pressure to prevent crushing of linoleum.

Merry Christmas Cards

Nail Keg Scuttle

Tools

1. Keyhole saw
2. Hammer
3. Tin snips
4. 1" paint brush
5. Hand drill and ⅛" twist drill
6. Pencil

Materials and Supplies

1. Paint and/or stain
2. Round or flat plastic lacing
3. Rough and fine sandpaper
4. Nail keg and end of orange crate

Procedure

Obtain an empty nail keg from a local hardware or building supply store. Use a hammer to remove nails from the metal rim supporting the open end of the keg. Remove metal rim and save the nails. Remove the wire band that is closest to the open end of the keg. With a pencil sketch the area of wood to be removed. Using a keyhole saw, carefully cut out along the pencil lines. Use rough and then fine sandpaper to smooth the cut edges. Sand the outside of the barrel to remove the splinters.

The end of an orange crate will supply material for the front supporting leg. Employ a scissors and paper to make a pattern of the leg. Transfer the shape of the leg to the wood, and cut out with keyhole saw and then sand smooth. Place the leg in proper position and nail securely from the inside of the keg.

Using tin snips, cut the overlapping joint from the metal rim removed from the top of the keg. Drill a small hole, one-half inch from each end of the metal rim. Place the metal rim in the desired position, and through each hole in the ends of the rim drive a nail into the keg; bend nail over on the inside. Paint or stain as desired. Wrap the handle with plastic lacing.

NAIL KEGS

Can be refashioned many different ways.

If you can salvage a nail keg, it
can become an instant success. Redesign
it and reshape it into a bright new
magazine holder, or a decorative
scuttle for your fireplace.

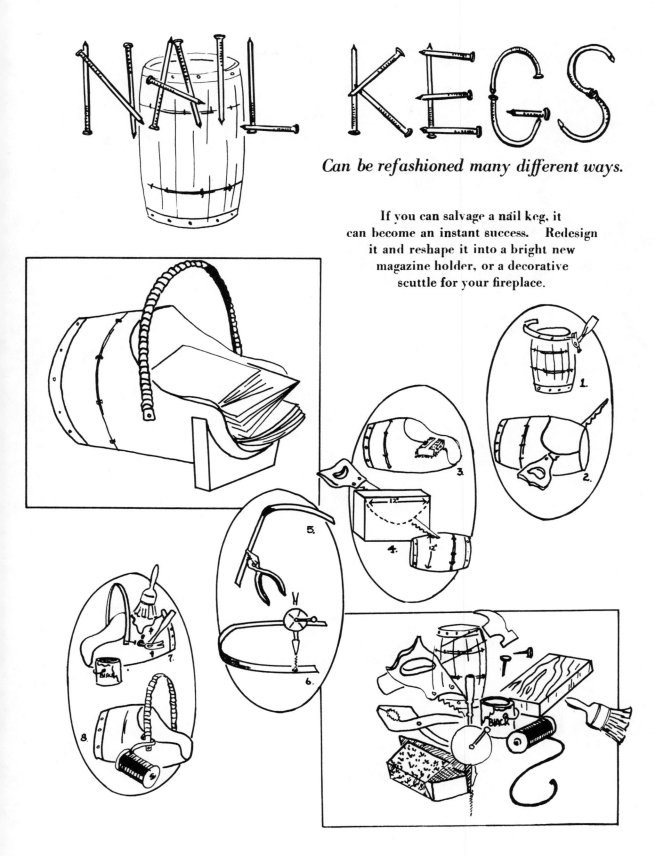

Stenciling

Tools

1. X-acto knife or single-edge razor blade
2. Stencil brushes (one for each color)

Materials and Supplies

1. 3 sheets of stencil paper
2. Cardboard
3. Crayons or colored pencils
4. Textile paints
5. Fabric
6. Masking tape
7. Rubber cement
8. Wiping cloth

Procedure

While a single-color stencil is easier to cut and print than a multi-colored stencil, for illustration purposes a three-color stencil has been selected to insure full coverage of the subject. Regardless of the number of colors used, the method employed is the same. The major difference is in the number of individual stencil sheets necessary for the complete design. Generally, for each color employed, a separate stencil sheet is necessary.

The illustration shows a three-color stencil of a rooster employing yellow, red, and black textile paint. The design desired is created full size on a piece of paper and the area covered by each color is carefully filled in, using the appropriate crayon or colored pencil. The sheet of paper containing the design should be pasted to a piece of cardboard that is slightly larger in size than the paper. Center a sheet of stencil paper over the design and hold in place with masking tape. Using a pencil, mark on the cardboard the upper left and lower left-hand corners of the stencil paper. Using X-acto knife or single-edge razor blade cut out all yellow areas of design on stencil paper (do not cut through cardboard). Remove masking tape and stencil from cardboard. Write on upper left-hand corner of stencil the word *yellow*. Take second sheet of stencil paper and place over design in the identical position that first stencil occupied. (Index marks placed on cardboard show locations of upper and lower left-hand corners of stencil paper.) Hold in place with masking tape and cut out the red areas of the design. Write the word *red* in upper left-hand corner of stencil and remove from cardboard.

The black stencil is cut in the same manner as the previously mentioned stencils, making certain to write the word *black* in the upper left-hand corner of the stencil. The marking of each stencil in the upper left-hand corner with the color to be used is important. This marking not only tells us the color to be employed with the specific stencil, but also locates the position the stencil occupies when it is to be printed.

The fabric to be stenciled should have been laundered at least once in order to remove the sizing from the material. (This washing permits the paint to penetrate into the fabric.) Gently stretch area of fabric to be stenciled over a piece of cardboard and hold in place with masking tape.

Carefully locate the position the design is to occupy on the fabric. Place the yellow cut stencils on the fabric in the correct position with the word *yellow* appearing in the upper left-hand corner. With a pencil, mark on the fabric the upper left and lower left-hand corners of the stencil sheet. Hold stencil sheet in place and dip stencil brush into yellow stencil paint. On scrap piece of paper work paint into brush. Employing an up and down motion (do not use brush strokes) dab yellow paint into cut out portions of design. Remove stencil from fabric and clean brush with wiping cloth. Locate position of red stencil and follow same procedure using black stencil. Permit material to dry for 24 hours and set paint by ironing on reverse side of fabric. When stenciling a repeat multi-color pattern, move from repeat to repeat pattern with same stencil and a single color at a time. Hold stencil steady.

Make
Fashion's
Gayest
Creations

Dancing Man

Tools

1. Coping saw
2. 4″ C-clamp
3. Hammer
4. Pencil
5. Scissors
6. Artist's brush
7. ½″ brush
8. Tempera paint
9. Shellac
10. Ruler

Materials and Supplies

1. Fine sandpaper
2. ⅝″ brads 20-gauge
3. Duco cement
4. ¼″ pine or soft wood
5. 2′ length of ⅜″ dowel or square stick
6. Drawing paper

Procedure

This project is constructed from nine pieces of one-quarter inch pine or other soft wood. The sides of an orange crate will provide an excellent source of lumber.

On a piece of construction paper lay out the individual parts, making certain that the knee and hip joints interlock three-eighths of an inch. This interlocking joint, when pinned with a nail, will provide free movement of the joints. Cut out paper patterns with a scissor. Place the pattern on the wood so that the grain of the wood runs lengthwise with all pieces. With a pencil trace an outline of required parts; remove patterns. Use a coping saw to

97

cut out pieces. Sandpaper all cut out parts. Using Duco cement and small brads, fasten the feet to the lower portion of the legs. Carefully fasten the knee and hip joints, using one nail for each joint. Fasten the arms by using a single nail at each shoulder joint. Flex all joints until free movement is accomplished. Drive a five-eighths inch brad through the center of the front of the body at the belt line into the end of the three-eighths inch dowel or stick; add Duco cement at this joint.

Using pencil, sketch detail as desired on the figure. Employ a fine brush and tempera paints to fill in the sketched areas. When this is dry, apply a thin coat of white shellac. When applying the shellac use long, even strokes without excessive brushing to prevent colors from running together.

Dry Point Etching

Tools

1. Scratch awl or needle in end of wooden dowel

Materials and Supplies

1. Celluloid about .020″ thick
2. Printer's ink
3. Plate oil
4. Wiping cloths
5. Paper
6. Tray
7. Water
8. Magazine
9. Discarded wash wringer
10. Paper towels

Procedure

Participants in this craft should be encouraged to develop "their own" designs. The picture developed should be drawn on paper; over this paper place a piece of celluloid. Using a scratch awl, carefully etch the lines of the picture or design into the celluloid. Shading in the picture is accomplished by merely scratching a series of parallel lines in the direction of the shadow. For a more intense shadow the lines are scratched deeper and closer together. For a really dark shadow the lines are scratched close together and at right angles to each other. When scratching your design it is well to remember that the drawing is being interpenetrated by a series of scratches. The closer the scratches, the darker the print. Using this technique it is possible to capture fine and accurate detail. Soak in clear water for twenty minutes several sheets of white drawing paper. Remove and shake excess water from paper. To remove additional surface moisture place a piece of paper toweling between each sheet of drawing paper.

Using the tip of your middle finger place a small amount of printing ink on the face of the celluloid that has been scratched. Using the tip of the same finger work the ink into the scratches. Place one drop of plate oil on the inked surface and with tip of finger spread evenly. Using palm of hand (DO NOT use wiping cloth) with a rotary motion wipe inked face clean. After each stroke across the plate with the palm of your hand, wipe ink off your hand on a cloth. Place inked celluloid plate in the middle of a magazine. Place moistened paper on the inked side of plate. Insert magazine in wash wringer (use great pressure) and squeeze. Remove print from inked plate and permit to dry. After each print re-ink plate. Be sure to employ the same procedure as previously described. Prints may be numbered in the sequence in which they were printed.

Add Artistic Touches

These dry point etchings can be used for inexpensive, decorative prints. A few simple steps, well within the abilities of an amateur, can reproduce any picture.

Drawing paper

PRINTER'S INK

PRINTER'S INK

BLACK

Collier's

Mugs

Tools

1. Glass cutter
2. Tin snips
3. Hand drill
4. ⅛" twist drill and ¼" twist drill
5. Coping saw
6. Smooth file
7. Slip joint pliers
8. Screw driver
9. 4" C-clamp
10. Hammer

Materials and Supplies

1. Cotton gloves
2. 60-grit emery powder
3. Fine emery cloth
4. Fine sandpaper
5. 20-gauge copper strips
6. Glass plate
7. Discarded bottle or glass jug
8. 1" wood board 12" x 12"
9. Alcohol
10. String
11. 1 piece of wood 1" x 1" x 12"
12. 2 pieces of wood 1" x 1" x 11"
13. 2, ¼" bolts with washers and wing nuts
14. 1" nails or screws
15. 2, 1" (8 x 32) brass bolts with nuts
16. Shellac
17. ½" brush

Procedure

The jig to hold the glass cutter is constructed from a flat one–inch board approximately 12 inches square. On adjacent sides of this board nail or screw two pieces of wood one by one inch. One piece should be 12 inches long and the other piece should be 11 inches long. Directly over the 11-inch piece of wood place another strip of wood one by one by 11 inches. Hold second strip of wood in place with C-clamp. Drill a one-quarter inch hole two inches in from each end and in the center of this strip. These holes go completely through both strips and also through the base. In these holes insert a one-quarter inch bolt with washers under the wing nuts (wing nuts should be placed on the one inch strip). Remove C-clamp. In the space between the two strips insert a glass cutter with the cutting wheel pointing towards the center of the square board. Obtain a discarded glass bottle. Place lip of bottle against corner formed by one–inch strips of wood. Adjust glass cutter in clamp so that cutting wheel is against bottle at point where cut is desired (cutter should be at right angles to side of bottle). Rotate bottle against glass cutter until a line is scored completely around bottle. Wrap five to eight turns of string around bottle three-eighths of an inch below scoring line. Saturate string with alcohol. Place upright on

ground or away from combustible materials, and ignite alcohol. Bottle will crack and break in two along scored line.

Place one-half teaspoon of 60-grit powdered emery on a flat glass plate. Add one spoonfull of water. On top of this plate and protecting your hands with a pair of cotton gloves, rotate the cut edge of the bottom portion of the bottle. When smooth use a small piece of emery paper and lightly smooth any remaining sharp edges or corners. Design and cut out handle from one-half inch wood. Lightly sandpaper until smooth. Make certain grain of wood runs lengthwise with handle. Cut two strips one-half inch wide of 20-gauge copper sheet stock and long enough to go around bottle with a one-half inch overlap. Using pliers, three-quarters of an inch of each end of these strips is bent in the same direction and at right angles to the strip. In the center of these four three-quarter inch tabs drill a one-eighth inch hole and place strips around mug in proper position with handle in place; mark location of holes to be drilled in handle. Using hand drill and one-eighth inch twist drill, drill holes in handle. Bolt strips to handle, using one-inch (8 by 32) brass bolts. Steel-wool copper strip and shellac handle. For aquarium, handle is not required.

MUGS *from* *discarded bottles !*

Big and husky

Beautiful and thrifty

Introducing a new craft with a double feature. For potted plants, small aquariums, and even vases.

Through the magic of this cutting method, an aristocrat of craft activities is born.

1.

2.

3.

4.

5.

6.

7.

8.

9.

10.

11.

12.

13.

ALCOHOL

EMERY POWDER

There's something new about the old bottle . . .

You'll never discard them again.

Selected Bibliography

Beskov, Elsa, and Anna Warburg, *Handwork Book for Children.* New York: Bridgman Publishing Company, Inc., 1940.

Birdsong, June, *Children's Rainy Day Play.* Philadelphia: Laurel Publishing Company, 1953.

Bjoland, Esther M., *Things to Make and Do.* Chicago: Standard Education Society, 1952.

Browne, Sibyl, *Art and Materials for the School.* New York: Progressive Education Association, 1943.

Carlson, Bernice W., *Make It Yourself: Handicraft for Boys and Girls.* New York: Abingdon-Cokesbury Press, 1950.

Crawford, Ida B., *Camp Counseling.* Philadelphia: W. B. Saunders Company, 1950.

Crocker, C. H., *Creative Carpentry.* Boston: Houghton, Mifflin Company, 1944.

———, *Let's Build.* Boston: Houghton, Mifflin Company, 1944.

Dank, Michael Carlton, *Adventures in Scrap Craft.* New York: Greenberg Publishing Company, 1947.

Dobbs, Ella V., *First Steps in Art and Handwork.* New York: The Macmillan Company, 1932.

Eckgren, B. L., and V. Fishel, *500 Live Ideas for the Grade Teacher.* Evanston, Illinois: Rowe, Peterson Company, 1952.

Ellsworth, Jaeger, *Easy Crafts.* New York: The Macmillan Company, 1947.

———, *Nature Crafts.* New York: The Macmillan Company, 1950.

Goss, Mary, and Dale Goss, *Do It Fun for Boys and Girls.* Peoria, Illinois: Charles A. Bennett and Company, 1950.

Graffam, Perry S., *Christmas Decorations Plus Cards, Gifts and Toys.* Chicago: General Publishing Company, Inc., 1949.

Grimm, Gretchen, and Katherine Skellas, *Craft Adventure for Children.* Milwaukee: Bruce Publishing Company.

Hayword, Charles H., *Carpentry for Beginners.* Philadelphia: Lippincott Company, 1951.

Hellier, Gay, *Indian Child Art.* London: Oxford University Press, 1951.

Henning, Viola, *Fun with Scraps.* Milwaukee: Bruce Publishing Company, 1947.

Holmes, K., and H. Collinson, *Child Art Grows Up.* London: Studio Publishing Co., 1952.

Horth, A. C., *Things for a Boy to Make.* New York: Lippincott Company, 1954.

Horwich, F. R., and Reinald Werrenrath, Jr., *Ding Dong School Book.* New York: Rand McNally, 1953.

———, *Miss Frances' All Day Long Book.* Chicago: Rand McNally, 1954.

Jacobson, Charlotte, *First Joiner Crafts.* Peoria, Illinois: Charles A. Bennett and Company, 1946.

Jenny, John H., *Recreation Education* (Introduction to). Philadelphia: W. B. Saunders Company, 1955.

Jordan, N., *Mother Goose Handicraft*. New York: Harcourt, Brace and Company, 1945.

Kay, J., and C. T. White, *Toys—Their Design and Construction*. Peoria, Illinois: Charles A. Bennett and Company, 1944.

Kephart, Horace, *Camping and Woodcraft*. New York: The Macmillan Company, 1939.

Lee, Tina, *What to do Now*. New York: Doubleday Company, 1946.

Leeming, Joseph, *Fun with Boxes*. Philadelphia: Lippincott Company, 1937.

———, *Fun with Fabrics*. Philadelphia: Lippincott Company, 1950.

———, *Fun with Wire*. Philadelphia: Lippincott Company, 1956.

———, *Holiday Craft and Fun*. Philadelphia: Lippincott Company, 1950.

———, *Papercrafts*. Philadelphia: Lippincott Company, 1949.

Lincoln, Martha, and Katherine Torrey, *The Workshop for Parents and Children*. Boston: Houghton, Mifflin Company, 1955.

MacLeish, Minnie, *Beginnings: Teaching Art to Children*. London: Studio Publishing Company, 1953.

Maginley, C. J., *Make It and Ride It*. New York: Harcourt, Brace and Company, 1949.

Mason, Bernard S., *Woodcraft*. New York: A. S. Barnes and Company, 1939.

Moore, F. C., C. H. Hamburger, and A. L. Kingcett, *Handicrafts for Elementary Schools*. Boston: Heath Publishing Company, 1953.

National Recreation Association, *Recreation and Park Yearbook*. New York: 1950.

Newkirk, Louis V., and W. H. Johnson, *The Industrial Arts Program*. New York: The Macmillan Company, 1948.

———, and La Vada Zutter, *Your Craft Book*. Scranton, Pennsylvania: International Textbook Company, 1948.

Oakley, W. K., *The Boy's Workshop Companion*. New York: Greenberg Publishing Company, 1952.

Oliver, Rita N., *Rain or Shine—Things to Make*. New York: Harcourt, Brace and Company, 1954.

Palestrant, Simon S., *Practical Papercraft*. New York: Home Crafts, 1950.

Robertson, S. M., *Creative Crafts in Education*. London: Routledge and Kegan Paul, 1952.

Shanklin, Margaret Eberhardt, *Use of Native Craft Materials*. Peoria, Illinois: Charles A. Bennett and Company, 1947.

Sprague, Curtiss, *How to Make It—Book of Crafts*. New York: Bridgman Publishing Company, Inc., 1941.

Wankelman, W., K. Richards, and M. Wigg, *Arts and Crafts for Elementary Teachers*. Boston: W. C. Brown Company, 1954.

Wolton, Harry, *Plastics for the Home Craftsman*. New York: McGraw-Hill Company, 1951.

C